"Simply adding a pattern made these cakes so much more fun."

I was wondering how to make Swiss roll cakes even more appealing to the eye when I had the idea of adding a pattern.

I went through a trial-and-error process to discover this very simple method! Just separate out a part of the batter and bake a pattern first. Adding this extra twist allows you to create all kinds of designs on a standard Swiss roll cake.

Strawberries, polka dots, hearts, argyle, etc...

These Deco Roll Cakes will make you happy the moment you see them, even before you can savor their flavors.

Junko

After developing a love of cooking, Junko studied nutrition and cuisine at a junior college. As a supplement to her main career as a graphic designer, she made pastries and introduced them on her blog, including recipes that use a bit of a twist for a more lovely presentation. Her blog is very popular, receiving over 10,000 hits per day. Junko's POV as a designer allows her to create original pastry ideas that garner much attention. Her blog: "A Little Extra Effort for Cute Cakes" http://ameblo.jp/chottono-kufu

"Deco ★ Cakes: Both the cook and the diners end up with smiles."

Of course these cakes are fun to eat, but they're also a joy to make! Your heart going pit-a-pat when drawing the patterns, the thrill of peeling the paper off the baked cake will lead you to want to make these cakes over and over again.

The batter is created using a fool-proof chiffon cake recipe that results in moist, fluffy cake. The batter is colored with cocoa powder and green tea powder, so it's guaranteed to be packed with flavor as well as great color!

Anyone who sees these cakes will give a surprised "Oh!" so they're perfect for dinner parties or as gifts.

Halloween, Christmas, Valentine's Day, birthdays...
Once you get the hang of making these cakes, you can have fun creating new designs for any occasion.
I'd be very pleased if these became staple recipes in your repertoire.

Junko

DECO ★ CAKES!

Swiss Rolls for Every Occasion

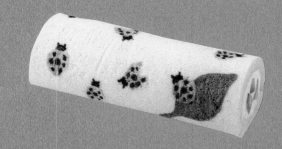

Junko

3 Secrets for
Delicious Deco ★ Cakes

1 Use fresh eggs and keep them refrigerated until right before use

Fresh eggs yield sturdy, good cake batter. Refrigerated egg whites are easier to whip. Fresh eggs simply taste all the better.

2 Don't let the baked cake dry out

Cover the baked cake with parchment paper to retain moistness and keep it from drying out. Dry, crumbly cake reduces deliciousness by half and also causes cracks when rolled up.

3 Real whipped cream is recommended

Rich, real cow's milk-based whipped cream goes best with light, fluffy chiffon cake. It melts in the mouth and is more flavorful than non-dairy versions.

So Many Exciting Patterns!

Contents

Prep tools you'll need

Cake pan

The cakes shown in this book are baked on a 25 x 25 cm walled baking sheet. You can also use the same amounts of ingredients listed in a 30 x 30 cm sheet, but the cake will be slightly thinner. A 30 x 35 cm baking sheet will yield a cake that's too thin, so a Swiss roll cake pan (25 x 25 cm) is recommended.

L: 30 x 30 cm (appx 12 x 12")
C: 25 x 25 cm (appx 10 x 10")
R: Swiss roll pan (25 x 25 cm).
Can be found in confectionery supply stores.

The cake on the right was made with a 25 x 25 cm pan. The left was made with a 30 x 30 cm pan. The 30^2 pan yields a thinner cake that requires more rolling. For cakes made with the 30^2 pan, use 4/5 C (200 ml) cream and 1 1/2 Tbsp (19 g) sugar.

Parchment Paper

a.k.a baking paper. Used to line baking sheets.

Scale

Measure out all ingredients before you start.

Measuring Cup

Used to measure oil and water.

Measuring Spoons

Used to measure small portions of cake flour, starch, etc.

Hand Mixer

Makes whipping egg whites into stiff peaks much easier than by hand.

Sifter

Used to combine flour and cocoa powder. A small strainer is also sufficient.

Bowls

Prep 3 bowls to make whipping egg yolks and whites easier. Use large bowl when whipping whites of 3 eggs.

Use small bowls or dishes for batter used to create patterns.

Rubber Spatula

Used to combine yolk batter and meringue or for pouring batter out of bowls and onto baking sheets.

Scraper

Used to smooth out the surface of batter once it's poured into a baking sheet. A rubber spatula can be substituted.

Cake Knife

Used to spread whipped cream frosting on the cake. A rubber spatula can be substituted.

Tools for making patterns
(Tools vary depending on pattern)

Spoon

Used to make simple patterns. Small spoons with tapered ends are easier to use.

Cornet

Used to make fine patterns. Made from parchment paper. A store-bought pastry piping bag can be substituted.

Fine-Point Brush

Used to create additional designs on finished cakes. Sold in dollar stores.

How to Make a Cornet

Cut parchment paper to 3/4".

Fold into a triangle.

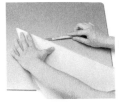

Cut.

Crease triangle in the center of the long edge.

Roll paper into a cone with the crease made above becoming the point.

Staple top edge to keep cone from unrolling.

Place cornet in a cup for easy handling when adding filling.

Once filling is added, fold down top.

Cut off the very tip.

Try piping to test.

Master the basics!
Pink Heart Deco ★ Cake

If you're just starting out, I recommend this basic cake.
The hearts can be made using a spoon.
The trick is to get both dark and light pinks for the hearts! ❤

Prep (yields one 25 x 25 cm (appx 10 x 10") cake)

Measure out all ingredients.

• Batter

☐ **4 eggs**
Medium (large is also acceptable)

↓

Divide eggs into 1 white, 3 whites, and 3 yolks. Discard 1 yolk.

☐ **1/3 C (65 g) sugar**

You can use superfine or regular granulated sugar. I use superfine here.

☐ **1/4 C (60 ml) water**

☐ **2 3/4 Tbsp (40 ml) vegetable oil**

☐ **Dash vanilla extract**

☐ **2/3 C (80 g) cake flour (for the cake)**

☐ **1 tsp cake flour (pattern) (divided in half)**

☐ **1 tsp corn starch**

☐ **1/8 tsp red food coloring**

Dilute with 1/4 tsp water before use. Natural, vegetable-based food dyes have a more subdued, subtle color.

• Syrup

☐ **2 1/2 tsp (10 g) granulated sugar**
☐ **1 1/3 Tbsp (20 ml) hot water**
☐ **1/2 Tbsp Grand Marnier***

*Optional

• Filling

☐ **2/3 C (150 ml) fresh cream**
☐ **3 1/3 tsp (14 g) sugar**
☐ **1/4 each banana, kiwi 1 slice yellow peach**

*Cream with 40% to 47% fat is recommended for whipping

Line baking sheet with parchment paper. Soak paper towel in oil and lightly grease paper.

Cut all 4 corners of paper and press into baking sheet.

Greasing the paper will prevent the pattern from sticking, making for a neater presentation.

Prep 2 spoons.

Small, tapered spoons are best suited for drawing patterns.

Preheat oven to 340°F (170°C)

Make yolk batter

1 Add 3 egg yolks to bowl and whisk. Add about half of sugar (35 g) and beat with hand mixer. Add water, oil and vanilla (in that order) and continue beating.

2 Sift in flour. Beat with hand mixer until sticky.

3 Add 2 tsp of yolk batter to 2 bowls. Add 1/2 tsp of cake flour to each bowl and stir well.

Half of sugar

1/4 C water

2 3/4 Tbsp oil

Dash vanilla extract

Once the water, oil and vanilla are incorporated, it's ready.

2/3 C cake flour

If you beat it to this point, the gluten will be developed, creating a springy cake that is crack-resistant when rolled. It's ready when the batter forms ribbons when the mixer is pulled away (sabayon).

2 tsp yolk batter

1/2 tsp cake flour

The additional flour makes the batter thicker, making it easier to draw patterns.

4 Dilute red food coloring with water and gradually add to one of the bowls from step **3** until light pink in color. Add slightly more coloring to the other bowl to create dark pink.

5 In a separate bowl, whisk 1 egg white until glossy and soft peaks form. Add a pinch of corn starch and continue whisking until stiff peaks form.

6 Stir in 1/3 of meringue to each of the pink batters.

Dash food coloring

1 egg white

Pinch corn starch

The difference in light and dark pinks should be close to the above photos. Food coloring dyes the batter instantly, so add gradually.

Egg whites beaten until stiff peaks form is called meringue. Adding corn starch helps the meringue retain its texture.

Stir well until smooth and no meringue lumps remain.

Draw pattern on paper

7 Using a spoon, drop dark pink batter into 1 cm (3/8") circles. Drop 2 circles next to each other, then use spoon to pull down batter into heart shapes.

Hold spoon perpendicular to paper surface and gently drop batter. Once you draw out the batter into heart shapes on the section closest to you, rotate the sheet and draw down the other half.

8 Use same method to draw light pink hearts. Pre-bake pattern at 340°F (170°C) for 1 minute. Bake immediately after drawing so they don't deflate.

They're ready when the surface is dried out as shown above. If they still seem too moist, keep baking in 30-second intervals until surface is dry. If the pattern is underbaked, it will run when the main cake batter is poured on top.

Whisk meringue

9 Add 3 eggs whites to bowl and beat with hand mixer. Once soft peaks form, whisk in remaining sugar left over from step **1** (30 g). Once glossy, add remaining corn starch and whisk until stiff peaks form.

Half of sugar

1 light tsp starch

The meringue is ready once stiff peaks form and it doesn't fall out even when the bowl is turned upside down.

Combine yolk batter and meringue

10 Combine remaining meringue left over from pattern batter and meringue from step **9** and stir in yolk batter 1/3 at a time. Stir thoroughly until smooth, with no meringue lumps.

The visible lumps are meringue. Break them up by slicing with the spatula. It's ready when the batter drips off the spatula in ribbons.

Pour batter onto baking sheet

11 Pour batter over pre-baked pattern on baking sheet. Smooth out surface. Whack sheet against work surface several times to remove air bubbles.

Banging on the underside of the sheet is also effective. This prevents air bubbles from disrupting the surface of the cake once baked.

Bake

12 Bake at 340°F (170°C) for 14 minutes or until a toothpick can be inserted and removed cleanly.

The cake should be a light brown color as shown above.

Flip over cake and allow to cool slightly

13 Cover surface of cake with new piece of parchment paper. Flip baking sheet containing cake over onto a cooling rack. Remove cake.

14 Peel parchment paper from surface right away, then replace paper and allow to cool slightly.

Make whipped cream filling

15 Add sugar to cream. Place bowl in ice water bath and whip until thickened.

Any type of wire cooling rack will do. The higher the rack, the faster the underside of the cake will cool.

The happy moment when you see the pattern! But if you don't replace the paper right away, the surface will dry out and the cake will crack when rolled up. Let cool for about 15 minutes or until no longer hot (but still warm) to the touch.

The percentage of fat in cream is what makes a difference in how easy it is to whip. Whip until cream thickens and stiff peaks form. If you over-whip, it will disintegrate, so be cautious.

Make syrup

16 Dissolve granulated sugar in hot water. Add Grand Marnier once cooled.

You can use superfine sugar, but granulated sugar gives a smoother mouthfeel.

Score cake and baste with syrup

17 Replace top parchment paper with fresh paper. Flip over so pattern is on the bottom. Remove parchment paper on top. Slice off front and back edges of cake at an angle.

Cutting off the ends makes for a nicer presentation once rolled up.

18 Lightly score surface of cake at 2 cm (3/4") intervals. Baste entire cake surface with syrup.

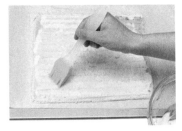

Scoring helps keep the cake surface from breaking when rolled up. Cover entire surface with syrup, but don't feel that you need to use up all of the syrup.

Add filling

19 Spread filling onto cake. Leave about 3 cm (1 1/4") at back edge unfrosted. Arrange fruit on cake.

Arrange the fruits at intervals shown above to create a pretty presentation when rolled up.

Roll up cake

20 Lift up front edge of cake along with parchment paper and roll forward over fruit into a circle. Press firmly and continue to roll up.

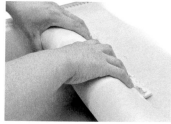

Lift up edge of parchment paper between thumbs and forefingers and tightly roll back. Mold firmly into shape, then unroll paper edge. Once entire cake is rolled up wrap paper around cake.

21 Twist ends of paper to fix in place. Refrigerate cake for at least 1 hour. This helps the flavors of the cake and filling to meld and become more delicious.

Twist up ends of paper like a candy wrapper. Refrigerate overnight for an even more flavorful cake.

Done!

22 Slice off ends of cake with a warm knife to clean up shape.

Warm knife by dousing with hot water. This allows you to slice cleanly through the filling.

If giving as a gift:

Use clear plastic wrap or film so the lovely pattern is visible. Finish with a ribbon that matches the colors of the cake.
→See p 51 for wrapping ideas.

Add decorations for more showiness

Use an extra touch of whipped cream, some fruit or chocolates to add extra glamour to the cake.
→See p 62 for decorating ideas.

Chocolate Heart Deco★Cake

This grown-up heart pattern is the second most popular recipe on our blog.
This is a chocolate variation on the heart cake for a flavor that's even popular
with the boys. Why not make this for Valentine's Day?

Prep

★ **Measure out all ingredients.**
★ **Line baking sheet with parchment paper and lightly grease with oil-soaked paper towel.**
★ **Preheat oven to 340ºF (170ºC).**   ★ **Prep 2 spoons.**

Ingredients (yields one 25 x 25 cm (appx 10 x 10") cake)

★ Batter
Eggs 4
   Divide into 1 white, 3 whites,
   and 3 yolks. Discard 1 yolk.
Sugar...................... 1/3 C (65 g)
Water .... 1/4 C (60 ml)
Vegetable oil.... 2 3/4 Tbsp (40 ml)
Dash vanilla extract

Cake flour (cake)..... 1/2 C (70 g)
Cake flour (pattern)............ 1 tsp
Corn starch .... 1 tsp
Red food coloring............ 1/8 tsp
   Dilute with appx 1/4 tsp
   water
Cocoa powder....... 2 Tbsp (10 g)

★ Syrup
Granulated sugar .... 2 1/2 tsp (10 g)
Hot water...... 1 1/3 Tbsp (20 ml)
Kirsch .... 1/2 Tbsp

★ Filling:
Fresh cream .... 2/3 C (150 ml)
Sugar.................... 3 1/3 tsp (14 g)
Strawberries................about 10

Make yolk batter

1 Add 3 egg yolks to bowl and whisk. Add half of sugar (35 g) and beat with hand mixer until lighter in color. Add water, oil and vanilla (in that order) and continue beating. Once mixed, sift in flour (for cake). Beat with hand mixer until sticky.

Make pattern

2 Add 2 tsp of yolk batter to a separate bowl. Stir in 1/2 tsp of flour.

3 Add another 2 tsp of yolk batter to another bowl. Stir in 1/2 tsp of cake flour. Gradually add diluted red food coloring until pink in color.

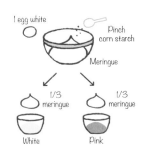

4 In a separate bowl, whisk 1 egg white with hand mixer. Add a pinch of corn starch to finish and continue whisking until stiff peaks form.

5 Stir 1/3 of meringue into the plain batter from step **2** (for white hearts). Stir 1/3 of meringue into the pink batter from step **3** (for pink hearts).

6 Using a spoon, drop white batter into 1 cm diam. circles onto paper-lined baking sheet. Drop 2 circles next to each other, then use spoon to pull down to a point, creating heart shapes. Bake for 1 minute.

7 Use same method to draw pink hearts. Drop any left over pattern batter to create a polka dot pattern. Bake for an additional 1 1/2 minutes.

Whisk meringue and make cake batter

8 Sift cocoa into remaining yolk batter from step 1. Stir thoroughly.

9 Add 3 egg whites to a bowl and beat with hand mixer. Once soft peaks form, whisk in remaining sugar from step 1 (30 g). Once glossy, add remaining corn starch (1 light tsp) and whisk until stiff peaks form.

10 Combine remaining meringue from steps **4** and **9** and stir into cocoa batter 1/3 at a time. Stir thoroughly until smooth, with no meringue lumps.

11 Pour batter over pre-baked pattern on baking sheet. Smooth out surface. Whack sheet against work surface several times to remove air bubbles.

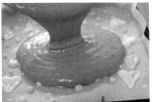

Bake

12 Bake at 340°F (170°C) for 14 minutes or until done. Cover surface of cake with parchment paper. Flip baking sheet containing cake over onto a cooling rack. Remove sheet.

13 Peel parchment paper from surface right away, then replace paper. Let cool slightly.

Make filling and roll up

14 Filling: Add sugar to cream and whip until thickened. Cut strawberries.

15 Syrup: Dissolve granulated sugar in hot water. Add Kirsch once cooled.

16 Flip cake over onto parchment paper so pattern is on the bottom. Slice off front and back edges of cake at an angle. Lightly score surface of cake at 2 cm (3/4") intervals. Baste with syrup. Spread filling onto cake from the back edge.

17 Arrange strawberry slices on cake. Lift up front edge of cake along with parchment paper and roll forward over strawberries. Press firmly and continue to roll up. Refrigerate cake for at least 1 hour.

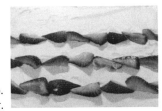

Flower Deco★Cake

**The flower petals are made with both light and dark pink batter,
but feel free to use just 1 color—it'll still be adorable!**

Prep

- ★ Measure out all ingredients.
- ★ Line baking sheet with parchment paper and lightly grease with oil-soaked paper towel.
- ★ Preheat oven to 340°F (170°C).   ★ Prep 2 spoons.

Ingredients (yields one 25 x 25 cm (appx 10 x 10") cake)

★ Batter

Eggs 4	Cake flour (cake)..... 2/3 C (80 g)
Divide into 1 white, 3 whites, and 3 yolks. Discard 1 yolk.	Cake flour (pattern)............1 tsp
	Corn starch ....1 tsp
Sugar...................... 1/3 C (65 g)	Red food coloring............1/8 tsp
Water .... 1/4 C (60 ml)	Dilute with appx 1/4 tsp water
Vegetable oil....2 3/4 Tbsp (40 ml)	
Dash vanilla extract	Cocoa powder.................1/4 tsp

★ Syrup

Granulated sugar .... 2 1/2 tsp (10 g)
Hot water...... 1 1/3 Tbsp (20 ml)
Grand Marnier .... 1/2 Tbsp

★ Filling:

Fresh cream .... 2/3 C (150 ml)
Sugar.................... 3 1/3 tsp (14 g)
Canned peaches.............3 slices

Make yolk batter

1 Add 3 egg yolks to bowl and whisk. Add half of sugar (35 g) and beat with hand mixer until lighter in color. Add water, oil and vanilla (in that order) and continue beating. Once mixed, sift in flour (for cake). Beat with hand mixer until sticky.

Make pattern

2 Add 2 tsp of yolk batter to 2 separate bowls. Stir in 1/2 tsp of cake flour (pattern) to each bowl.

3 Dilute red food coloring with water and gradually add to 1 bowl from step **2** until light pink in color. Add slightly more coloring to the other bowl to create dark pink.

4 Add 1 tsp of yolk batter to another bowl. Gradually stir in cocoa powder until batter is brown.

5 In a separate bowl, whisk 1 egg white with hand mixer. Add a pinch of corn starch to finish and continue whisking until stiff peaks form.

6 Stir 1/3 of meringue into both batters from step **3** (for flower petals). Stir 3 Tbsp of meringue into batter from step **4** (for pistils).

7 Using a spoon, drop brown batter into 1 cm diam. circles onto paper-lined baking sheet. Bake for 1 minute.

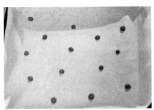

8 Drop light and dark pink batters in circles around brown dots then spread into petal shapes with spoon tip (see photo). Drop any remaining batter into open areas and pull into petals. Bake for an additional 1 1/2 minutes.

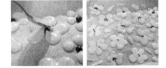

Whisk meringue and make cake batter

9 Add 3 egg whites to a bowl and beat with hand mixer. Once soft peaks form, whisk in remaining sugar from step **1** (30 g). Once glossy, add remaining corn starch (1 light tsp) and whisk until stiff peaks form.

10 Combine remaining meringue from steps **5** and **9** and stir 1/3 at a time into yolk batter from step **1**. Stir thoroughly until smooth, with no meringue lumps.

11 Pour batter over pre-baked pattern on baking sheet. Smooth out surface. Whack sheet against work surface several times to remove air bubbles.

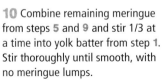

Bake

12 Bake at 340°F (170°C) for 14 minutes or until done. Cover surface of cake with parchment paper. Flip baking sheet containing cake over onto a cooling rack. Remove sheet.

13 Peel parchment paper from surface right away, then replace paper and allow to cool slightly.

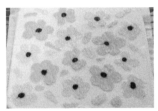

Make filling and roll up

14 Filling: Add sugar to cream and whip until thickened. Quarter each peach slice into wedges.

15 Syrup: Dissolve granulated sugar in hot water. Add Grand Marnier once cooled.

16 Flip cake over onto parchment paper so pattern is on the bottom. Slice off front and back edges of cake at an angle. Lightly score surface of cake at 2 cm (3/4") intervals. Baste with syrup. Spread filling onto cake from the back edge.

17 Arrange peaches slices on cake. Lift up front edge of cake along with parchment paper and roll forward over peaches. Press firmly and continue to roll up. Refrigerate cake for at least 1 hour.

Abstract Coffee Deco★Cake

Drizzling random lines creates a surprisingly grown-up, chic-looking pattern.
Coffee-flavored cake is my absolute favorite.

Prep

- ★ Measure out all ingredients.
- ★ Line baking sheet with parchment paper and lightly grease with oil-soaked paper towel.
- ★ Preheat oven to 340°F (170°C).   ★ Prep 2 spoons.

Ingredients (yields one 25 x 25 cm (appx 10 x 10") cake)

★ Batter

Eggs 4
   Divide into 1 white, 3 whites,
   and 3 yolks. Discard 1 yolk.
Sugar....................... 1/3 C (65 g)
Vegetable oil....2 3/4 Tbsp (40 ml)
Dash vanilla extract

Coffee A

⌐ Instant coffee................. 2 tsp
| Hot water........ 2 Tbsp (30 ml)
└ Milk .... 2 Tbsp (30 ml)
Dissolve coffee in hot water,
then add milk
Cake flour (cake)..... 2/3 C (80 g)
Cake flour (pattern) ..... 1 1/2 tsp
Corn starch ....1 tsp

Coffee B

⌐ Instant coffee................. 2 tsp
└ Hot water....................... 1 tsp
Add 1 tsp hot water to instant
coffee and stir with rubber
spatula until dissolved.

★ Syrup:
Granulated sugar .... 2 1/2 tsp (10 g)
Hot water...... 1 1/3 Tbsp (20 ml)
Instant coffee .... 1 tsp

★ Filling:
Fresh cream .... 2/3 C (150 ml)
Sugar.................... 3 1/3 tsp (14 g)
Banana..1

Make yolk batter

1 Add 3 egg yolks to bowl and whisk. Add half of sugar (35 g) and beat with hand mixer until lighter in color. Add Coffee A, oil and vanilla (in that order) and continue beating. Once mixed, sift in flour (for cake). Beat with hand mixer until sticky.

Make pattern

2 Add 2 tsp of yolk batter to 2 separate bowls.

3 Stir in 1/2 tsp of cake flour and 1/4 tsp Coffee B to 1 bowl from step **2** to make light brown batter. Add 1 tsp cake flour and remaining Coffee B to other bowl to create dark brown batter.

4 In a separate bowl, whisk 1 egg white with hand mixer. Add a pinch of corn starch to finish and continue whisking until stiff peaks form.

5 Stir 1/3 of meringue into both batters from step **3**.

6 Using a spoon, drizzle random lines with light brown batter onto paper-lined baking sheet. Bake for 1 minute.

7 Drizzle random lines with dark brown batter over light brown lines. Bake for an additional 1 minute.

Whisk meringue and make cake batter

8 Add 3 egg whites to a bowl and beat with hand mixer. Once soft peaks form, whisk in remaining sugar from step **1** (30 g). Once glossy, add remaining corn starch (1 light tsp) and whisk until stiff peaks form.

9 Combine remaining meringue from steps **4** and **8** and stir 1/3 at a time into batter from step **1**. Stir thoroughly until smooth, with no meringue lumps.

10 Pour batter over pre-baked pattern on baking sheet. Smooth out surface. Whack sheet against work surface several times to remove air bubbles.

Bake

11 Bake at 340ºF (170ºC) for 14 minutes or until done. Cover surface of cake with parchment paper. Flip baking sheet containing cake over onto a cooling rack. Remove sheet.

12 Peel parchment paper from surface right away, then replace paper. While still warm, place in a ziplock bag, seal* and let cool slightly.

Make filling and roll up

13 Filling: Add sugar to cream and whip until thickened.

14 Syrup: Dissolve granulated sugar and instant coffee in hot water. Let cool.

15 Flip cake over onto parchment paper so pattern is on the bottom. Slice off front and back edges of cake at an angle. Lightly score surface of cake at 2 cm (3/4") intervals. Baste with syrup. Spread filling onto cake from the back edge.

16 Arrange banana slices on cake. Lift up front edge of cake along with parchment paper and roll forward over banana. Press firmly and continue to roll up. Refrigerate cake for at least 1 hour.

*Since coffee cake crumbles easily, cooling in a plastic bag retains moisture.

Teddy Bear Deco★Cake

**Place paper pattern on baking sheet then spoon batter over pattern to create the design.
Have fun finishing the cake by painting on the eyes and mouth to make the faces
all the more adorable. (Pattern p 78)**

Prep

★ Measure out all ingredients.
★ Place paper pattern on baking sheet. Top with parchment paper
   and lightly grease with oil-soaked paper towel.
★ Preheat oven to 340°F (170°C).   ★ Prep 2 spoons.
★ Prep fine brush (see p 9).

Ingredients (yields one 25 x 25 cm (appx 10 x 10") cake)

★ Batter

Eggs 4
   Divide into 1 white, 3 whites,
   and 3 yolks. Discard 1 yolk.
Sugar...................... 1/3 C (65 g)
Water .... 1/4 C (60 ml)
Vegetable oil ....2 3/4 Tbsp (40 ml)
Dash vanilla extract

Cake flour (cake) ..... 1/2 C (70 g)
Cake flour (pattern) ... 1/2 heaping tsp
Corn starch .... 1 tsp
Cocoa powder .... 2 Tbsp (10 g)

★ Syrup:

Granulated sugar .... 2 1/2 tsp (10 g)
Hot water ...... 1 1/3 Tbsp (20 ml)
Rum .... 1 tsp

★ Filling:

Fresh cream .... 2/3 C (150 ml)
Sugar..................... 3 1/3 tsp (14 g)
Banana.. 1

★ For drawing faces

Black cocoa powder .... 1 tsp
Hot water .... 1 tsp
   Black cocoa powder is
   very dark cocoa used in
   confectionery. Regular cocoa
   powder is OK, too.

Make yolk batter

1 Add 3 egg yolks to bowl and whisk. Add half of sugar (35 g) and beat with hand mixer until lighter in color. Add water, oil and vanilla (in that order) and continue beating. Once mixed, sift in flour (for cake). Beat with hand mixer until sticky.

Make pattern

2 Add 2 tsp of yolk batter to a separate bowl. Stir in 1/2 tsp of cake flour (pattern).

3 Add 1 tsp yolk batter to another bowl. Stir in 1/8 tsp cake flour and 1/8 tsp from listed amount of cocoa powder to make light brown batter.

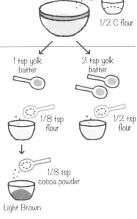

4 In a separate bowl, whisk 1 egg white with hand mixer. Add a pinch of corn starch to finish and continue whisking until stiff peaks form.

5 Stir 1/3 of meringue into batter from step **3** (for white batter). Stir 3 Tbsp of meringue into batter from step **4** (for light brown batter).

6 On lined baking sheet, draw teddy bears' muzzles with brown batter from step **5**. Use a spoon to fill in muzzle sections with batter. Bake for 1 minute.

7 Fill in teddy bears' heads with white batter from step **5**. Bake for an additional 1 minute.

Whisk meringue and make cake batter

8 Sift cocoa powder into remaining yolk batter from step **1**. Stir thoroughly.

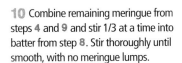

9 Add 3 egg whites to a bowl and beat with hand mixer. Once soft peaks form, whisk in remaining sugar from step **1** (30 g). Once glossy, add remaining corn starch (1 light tsp) and whisk until stiff peaks form.

10 Combine remaining meringue from steps **4** and **9** and stir 1/3 at a time into batter from step **8**. Stir thoroughly until smooth, with no meringue lumps.

11 Pour batter over pre-baked pattern on baking sheet. Smooth out surface. Whack sheet against work surface several times to remove air bubbles.

Bake

12 Bake at 340°F (170°C) for 14 minutes or until done. Cover surface of cake with parchment paper. Flip baking sheet containing cake over onto a cooling rack. Remove sheet.

13 Peel parchment paper from surface right away, then replace paper and allow to cool slightly.

Make filling and roll up

14 Filling: Add sugar to cream and whip until thickened.

15 Syrup: Dissolve granulated sugar in hot water. Add rum once cooled.

16 Flip cake over onto parchment paper so pattern is on the bottom. Slice off front and back edges of cake at an angle. Lightly score surface of cake at 2 cm (3/4") intervals. Baste with syrup. Spread filling onto cake from the back edge.

17 Arrange banana on cake. Lift up front edge of cake along with parchment paper and roll forward over banana. Press firmly and continue to roll up. Refrigerate cake for at least 1 hour. To finish, dissolve black cocoa powder in hot water and paint eyes, noses and mouths onto teddy bears' faces.

27

Prep

- ★ Measure out all ingredients.
- ★ Place paper pattern on baking sheet. Top with parchment paper and lightly grease with oil-soaked paper towel.
- ★ Preheat oven to 340°F (170°C).
- ★ Make cornet out of parchment paper (see p 9).

Ingredients
(yields one 25 x 25 cm (appx 10 x 10") cake)

★ Batter
Eggs 4
   Divide into 1 white, 3 whites, and
   3 yolks. Discard 1 yolk.
Sugar.. 1/3 C (65 g)
Water ....1/4 C (60 ml)
Vegetable oil................. 2 3/4 Tbsp (40 ml)
Dash vanilla extract
Cake flour (cake)..................... 1/2 C (70 g)
Cake flour (pattern)......................... 1/2 tsp
Corn starch .... 1 tsp
Cocoa powder....................... 2 Tbsp (10 g)

★ Syrup:
Granulated sugar ....2 1/2 tsp (10 g)
Hot water...................... 1 1/3 Tbsp (20 ml)
Rum .... 1 tsp

★ Filling:
Fresh cream ....2/3 C (150 ml)
Sugar.................................... 3 1/3 tsp (14 g)

Giraffe Deco★Cake

Made with the same chocolate batter as the Chocolate Heart Deco Cake. Create the pattern by using a cornet and piping along the paper pattern provided on p 79.

Make yolk batter

1 Add 3 egg yolks to bowl and whisk. Add half of sugar (35 g) and beat with hand mixer until lighter in color. Add water, oil and vanilla (in that order) and continue beating. Once mixed, sift in flour (for cake). Beat with hand mixer until sticky.

Make pattern

2 Add 1 Tbsp of yolk batter to a separate bowl. Stir in 1/2 tsp of cake flour (pattern).

3 In a separate bowl, whisk 1 egg white with hand mixer. Add a pinch of corn starch to finish and continue whisking until stiff peaks form.

4 Stir 2/3 of meringue into batter from step **2**. Add to cornet.

5 On lined baking sheet, pipe giraffe pattern with cornet. Since the lines are thin, make sure they have height.

6 Bake for 1 1/2 minutes.

Whisk meringue and make cake batter

7 Sift cocoa powder into remaining yolk batter from step **1**. Stir thoroughly.

8 Add 3 egg whites to a bowl and beat with hand mixer. Once soft peaks form, whisk in remaining sugar from step **1** (30 g). Once glossy, add remaining corn starch (1 light tsp) and whisk until stiff peaks form.

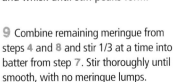

9 Combine remaining meringue from steps **4** and **8** and stir 1/3 at a time into batter from step **7**. Stir thoroughly until smooth, with no meringue lumps.

10 Pour batter over pre-baked pattern on baking sheet. Smooth out surface. Whack sheet against work surface several times to remove air bubbles.

Bake

11 Bake at 340°F (170°C) for 14 minutes or until done. Cover surface of cake with parchment paper. Flip baking sheet containing cake over onto a cooling rack. Remove sheet.

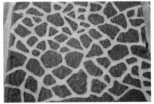

12 Peel parchment paper from surface right away, then replace paper and allow to cool slightly.

Make filling and roll up

13 Filling: Add sugar to cream and whip until thickened.

14 Syrup: Dissolve granulated sugar in hot water. Add rum once cooled.

15 Flip cake over onto parchment paper so pattern is on the bottom. Slice off front and back edges of cake at an angle. Lightly score surface of cake at 2 cm (3/4") intervals. Baste with syrup. Spread filling onto cake from the back edge.

16 Lift up front edge of cake along with parchment paper and roll forward. Press firmly and continue to roll up. Refrigerate cake for at least 1 hour.

Dalmatian Deco★Cake

Draw the black spots with black cocoa powder.
Make the spots slightly irregular to make them look like a Dalmatian's coat. Create bigger spots to create a cow pattern.

Variation

Cow Pattern

You can make a cow cake using the same recipe. Make a smaller number of bigger spots to create the effect.

Prep

- ★ Measure out all ingredients.
- ★ Place paper pattern on baking sheet. Top with parchment paper and lightly grease with oil-soaked paper towel.
- ★ Preheat oven to 340ºF (170ºC).
- ★ Make cornet out of parchment paper (see p 9).

Ingredients (yields one 25 x 25 cm (appx 10 x 10") cake)

★ Batter		★ Syrup	★ Filling
Eggs 4	Dash vanilla extract	Granulated sugar .... 2 1/2 tsp (10 g)	Fresh cream .... 2/3 C (150 ml)
Divide into 1 white, 3 whites,	Cake flour (cake)..... 2/3 C (80 g)	Hot water...... 1 1/3 Tbsp (20 ml)	Sugar...................... 3 1/3 tsp (14 g)
and 3 yolks. Discard 1 yolk.	Corn starch .... 1 tsp	Grand Marnier .... 1/2 Tbsp	Kiwi, banana................ 1/4 each
Sugar...................... 1/3 C (65 g)	Black cocoa powder........... 1 tsp		Canned yellow peach....... 1 slice
Water .... 1/4 C (60 ml)			
Vegetable oil....2 3/4 Tbsp (40 ml)			

Make yolk batter

1 Add 3 egg yolks to bowl and whisk. Add half of sugar (35 g) and beat with hand mixer until lighter in color. Add water, oil and vanilla (in that order) and continue beating. Once mixed, sift in flour (for cake). Beat with hand mixer until sticky.

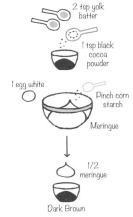

3 yolks

1/2 sugar (35 g)

1/4 C water

Dash vanilla extract

2 3/4 Tbsp oil

2/3 C flour

Make pattern

2 Add 2 tsp of yolk batter to a separate bowl. Stir in 1 tsp black cocoa powder.

2 tsp yolk batter

1 tsp black cocoa powder

3 In a separate bowl, whisk 1 egg white with hand mixer. Add a pinch of corn starch to finish and continue whisking until stiff peaks form.

1 egg white

Pinch corn starch

Meringue

4 Stir 1/3 of meringue into batter from step **2**. Add to cornet.

1/2 meringue

Dark Brown

5 On lined baking sheet, pipe Dalmatian pattern with cornet. Since the spots might fall off easily, apply thick amounts of batter. Bake for 1 1/2 minutes.

Whisk meringue and make cake batter

6 Add 3 egg whites to a bowl and beat with hand mixer. Once soft peaks form, whisk in remaining sugar from step **1** (30 g). Once glossy, add remaining corn starch (1 light tsp) and whisk until stiff peaks form.

3 egg whites

1/2 sugar (30 g)

Meringue

1 light tsp corn starch

Meringue left over from step 3

7 Combine remaining meringue from steps **3** and **6** and stir 1/3 at a time into batter from step **1**. Stir thoroughly until smooth, with no meringue lumps.

8 Pour batter over pre-baked pattern on baking sheet. Smooth out surface. Whack sheet against work surface several times to remove air bubbles.

Bake

9 Bake at 340°F (170°C) for 14 minutes or until done. Cover surface of cake with parchment paper. Flip baking sheet containing cake over onto a cooling rack. Remove sheet.

340°F 14 mins

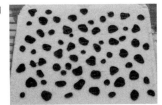

10 Peel parchment paper from surface right away, then replace paper and allow to cool slightly.

Make filling and roll up

11 Filling: Add sugar to cream and whip until thickened. Cut fruit.

12 Syrup: Dissolve granulated sugar in hot water. Add Grand Marnier once cooled.

13 Flip cake over onto parchment paper so pattern is on the bottom. Slice off front and back edges of cake at an angle. Lightly score surface of cake at 2 cm (3/4") intervals. Baste with syrup. Spread filling onto cake from the back edge.

14 Arrange fruit on top of cake. Lift up front edge of cake along with parchment paper and roll forward over fruit. Press firmly and continue to roll up. Refrigerate cake for at least 1 hour.

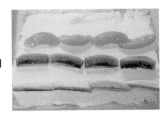

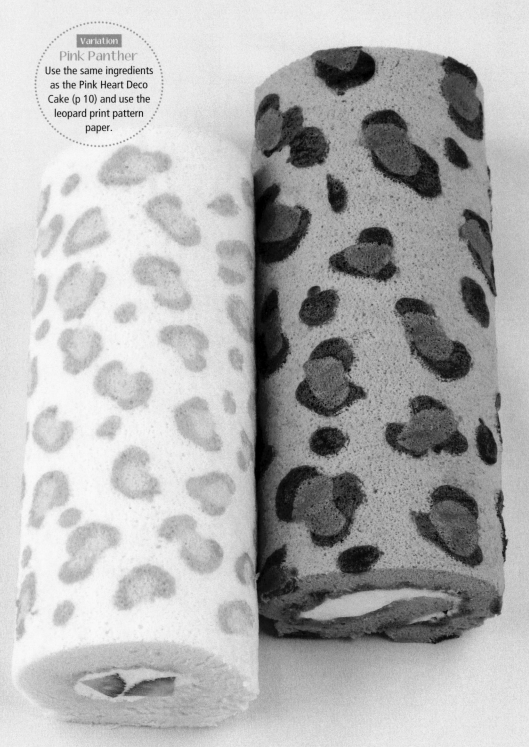

Variation

Pink Panther

Use the same ingredients as the Pink Heart Deco Cake (p 10) and use the leopard print pattern paper.

Prep

★ Measure out all ingredients.
★ Line baking sheet with parchment paper and lightly grease with oil-soaked paper towel.
★ Preheat oven to 340°F (170°C).
★ Prep 2 spoons.

Ingredients

(yields one 25 x 25 cm (appx 10 x 10") cake

★ **Batter**

Eggs 4
    Divide into 1 white, 3 whites, and 3 yolks. Discard 1 yolk.
Sugar ....1/3 C (65 g)
Vegetable oil ...... 2 3/4 Tbsp (40 ml)
Dash vanilla extract
Coffee A
   ⌐ Instant coffee .... 2 tsp
   | Hot water ....2 Tbsp (30 ml)
   ⌐ Milk ....2 Tbsp (30 ml)
   Dissolve coffee in hot water, then add milk.
Cake flour (cake) ....2/3 C (80 g)
Cake flour (pattern) .... 1 1/2 tsp
Corn starch .... 1 tsp
Coffee B
   ⌐ Instant coffee .... 2 tsp
   ⌐ Hot water .... 1 tsp
   Add 1 tsp hot water to instant coffee and stir with rubber spatula until dissolved.

- -

★ **Syrup**

Granulated sugar ....2 1/2 tsp (10 g)
Hot water ....1 1/3 Tbsp (20 ml)
Instant coffee .... 1 tsp

- -

★ **Filling**

Fresh cream ....2/3 C (150 ml)
Sugar ....3 1/3 tsp (14 g)

Leopard Deco★Cake

Leopard print is very popular with my friends from western Japan.
The coffee-flavored version looks and tastes more sophisticated.
Try the pink version for a very girly twist.

Make yolk batter

1 Add 3 egg yolks to bowl and whisk. Add half of sugar (35 g) and beat with hand mixer until lighter in color. Add Coffee A, oil and vanilla (in that order) and continue beating. Once mixed, sift in flour (for cake). Beat with hand mixer until sticky.

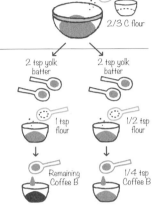

Make pattern

2 Add 2 tsp of yolk batter to 2 separate bowls.

3 Stir in 1/2 tsp of cake flour and 1/4 tsp Coffee B to 1 bowl from step **2** to make light brown batter. Add 1 tsp cake flour and remaining Coffee B to other bowl to create dark brown batter.

4 In a separate bowl, whisk 1 egg white with hand mixer. Add a pinch of corn starch to finish and continue whisking until stiff peaks form.

5 Stir 1/3 of meringue into both batters from step **3**.

6 Using a spoon, drop light brown batter on paper-lined baking sheet to make light leopard spots. Bake for 1 minute. Drop dark brown batter around light brown batter (appx 2/3 of the way around each spot) to make dark parts of spots. Drop circles of dark brown batter onto open spaces. Bake for 1 minute.

Whisk meringue and make cake batter

7 Add 3 egg whites to a bowl and beat with hand mixer. Once soft peaks form, whisk in remaining sugar from step **1** (30 g). Once glossy, add remaining corn starch (1 light tsp) and whisk until stiff peaks form.

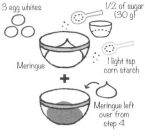

8 Combine remaining meringue from steps **4** and **7** and stir 1/3 at a time into batter from step **1**. Stir thoroughly until smooth, with no meringue lumps.

9 Pour batter over pre-baked pattern on baking sheet. Smooth out surface. Whack sheet against work surface several times to remove air bubbles.

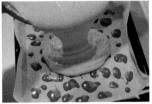

Bake

10 Bake at 340°F (170°C) for 14 minutes or until done. Cover surface of cake with parchment paper. Flip baking sheet containing cake over onto a cooling rack. Remove sheet.

11 Peel parchment paper from surface right away, then replace paper. While still warm, place in a ziplock bag, seal* and let cool slightly.

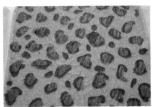

Make filling and roll up

12 Filling: Add sugar to cream and whip until thickened.

13 Syrup: Dissolve granulated sugar and instant coffee in hot water. Let cool.

14 Flip cake over onto parchment paper so pattern is on the bottom. Slice off front and back edges of cake at an angle. Lightly score surface of cake at 2 cm (3/4") intervals. Baste with syrup. Spread filling onto cake from the back edge.

15 Lift up front edge of cake along with parchment paper and roll forward. Press firmly and continue to roll up. Refrigerate cake for at least 1 hour.

*Since coffee cake crumbles easily, cooling in a plastic bag retains moisture.

Zebra Deco★Cake

This is a twist on the recipe for the Dalmation cake.
Draw pattern with a cornet.

Prep

★ See instructions for previous Deco Cakes.

Ingredients (yields one 25 cm² (10"²) cake)

★ Batter

Eggs 4
Divide into 1 white,
3 whites, and 3
yolks. Discard 1
yolk.
Sugar...... 1/3 C (65 g)
Water... 1/4 C (60 ml)
Vegetable oil
.....2 3/4 Tbsp (40 ml)
Dash vanilla extract
Cake flour (cake)
.... 2/3 C (80 g)
Corn starch .... 1 tsp
Black cocoa powder
...................................1 tsp

★ Syrup

Granulated sugar
..........2 1/2 tsp (10 g)
Hot water
..... 1 1/3 Tbsp (20 ml)
Kirsch .... 1/2 Tbsp

★ Filling

Fresh cream
.... 2/3 C (150 ml)
Granulated sugar
..........3 1/3 tsp (14 g)
Strawberries
...................about 10

Make yolk batter

1 Add 3 egg yolks to bowl and whisk. Add half of sugar (35 g) and beat with hand mixer until lighter in color. Add water, oil and vanilla (in that order) and continue beating. Once mixed, sift in flour (for cake). Beat with hand mixer until sticky.

Make pattern

2 Add 1 Tbsp of yolk batter to a separate bowl. Stir in 1 tsp black cocoa powder.

3 In a separate bowl, whisk 1 egg white with hand mixer. Add a pinch of corn starch to finish and continue whisking until stiff peaks form.

4 Stir 1/2 of meringue into batter from step **2**. Add to cornet.

5 On lined baking sheet, pipe zebra pattern with cornet. Since the stripes might fall off easily, apply thick amounts of batter. Bake for 1 1/2 minutes.

Whisk meringue and make cake batter

6 Add 3 egg whites to a bowl and beat with hand mixer. Once soft peaks form, whisk in remaining sugar from step **1** (30 g). Once glossy, add remaining corn starch (1 light tsp) and whisk until stiff peaks form.

7 Combine remaining meringue from steps **3** and **6** and stir 1/3 at a time into batter from step 1. Stir thoroughly until smooth, with no meringue lumps.

8 Pour batter over pre-baked pattern on baking sheet. Smooth out surface. Whack sheet against work surface several times to remove air bubbles.

Bake

9 Bake at 340ºF (170ºC) for 14 minutes or until done. Cover surface of cake with parchment paper. Flip baking sheet containing cake over onto a cooling rack. Remove sheet.

10 Peel parchment paper from surface right away, then replace paper and allow to cool slightly.

Make filling and roll up

11 Filling: Add sugar to cream and whip until thickened. Cut strawberries into wedges.

12 Syrup: Dissolve granulated sugar in hot water. Add Kirsch once cooled.

13 Flip cake over onto parchment paper so pattern is on the bottom. Slice off front and back edges of cake at an angle. Lightly score surface of cake at 2 cm (3/4") intervals. Baste with syrup. Spread filling onto cake from the back edge.

14 Arrange strawberries on top of cake. Lift up front edge of cake along with parchment paper and roll forward over strawberries. Press firmly and continue to roll up. Refrigerate cake for at least 1 hour.

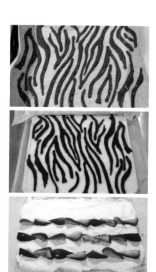

Delicious cake and filling combos

The decisive factor for delicious deco rolls is the combination of cake, filling and the liqueur used in the syrup. As for the fruit, just memorize some basic tips and you'll end up with a great cake filling even if you don't follow the recipe. Discover your own favorite flavor combinations!

These fruits are best suited for filling Swiss roll cakes

I recommend strawberries, bananas, kiwis and mangoes. Canned fruit, available year-round, works well alone or in combination with other fruit, which is convenient. Of course, you can skip the fruit and just use whipped cream, too.

When using combinations of fruit, cut them all to similar widths so the cross-sections look pretty. Strawberries can be used whole.

Bananas are best with brown batters

Bananas go great with coffee and chocolate cakes. Use plain whipped cream or chocolate cream for the filling. I recommend rum syrup for chocolate cakes and instant coffee syrup for coffee flavored cakes.

Bananas for chocolate

Baste the cuts on the banana with sugar water to prevent oxidization.

Use anko bean paste as filling for green tea cake.

Tangy fruit doesn't go very well with the slightly astringent flavor of green tea cake. The combination of whipped cream filling and anko bean paste gives a fresh Japanese twist.

These are sweet boiled azuki beans

You can find sweet boiled azuki beans in finer grocery stores. If you don't like azuki beans, simply use whipped cream frosting alone.

These liqueurs complement fruit flavors.

Kirsch (cherry brandy) is the best match for strawberries. Rum is perfect for the rich flavors of bananas. Since rum has a stronger flavor and aroma than other liqueurs, the recipes calling for rum use less than other liqueurs. Use orange-infused Grand Marnier for other fruit.

The syrup also helps to keep the cake from drying out, so don't forget it!

Small Polka Dots Deco★Cake

I used a cornet to create small dots of different colored batter.
Different combinations of colors give different impressions,
so try using all kinds of colors.

Variation

Chocolate & Polka Dots

Use white and pink batter for the dots and chocolate batter for the cake. See Chocolate Heart Deco Cake (p 20) for ingredients.

Prep

★ Measure out all ingredients.
★ Line baking sheet with parchment paper and lightly grease with oil-soaked paper towel.
★ Preheat oven to 340ºF (170ºC).
★ Make cornet out of parchment paper (see p 9).

Ingredients (yields one 25 x 25 cm (appx 10 x 10") cake)

★ Batter

Eggs 5
   Divide into 1 white, 4 whites,
   and 1 yolk. Discard 4 yolks.
Sugar..................... 5 Tbsp (60 g)
Water .... 1/4 C (60 ml)
Vegetable oil .... 3 Tbsp (45 ml)
Dash vanilla extract

Cake flour (cake)..... 2/3 C (80 g)
Cake flour (pattern)......... 1/4 tsp
Corn starch .... 1 tsp
Black cocoa powder .... 1/4 tsp
   (Or regular cocoa powder)
Red food coloring............ 1/8 tsp
   Dilute with appx 1/4 tsp water

★ Syrup

Granulated sugar .... 2 1/2 tsp (10 g)
Hot water...... 1 1/3 Tbsp (20 ml)
Kirsch .... 1/2 Tbsp

★ Filling

Fresh cream .... 2/3 C (150 ml)
Sugar..................... 3 1/3 tsp (14 g)
Strawberries............................ 4
Kiwi... 1/4
Banana.................................... 1/2

Make yolk batter

1 Add 1 egg yolk to bowl and whisk. Add half of sugar (30 g) and 1/2 of oil (20 ml) and beat with hand mixer until lighter in color. Add water, remaining oil and vanilla (in that order) and continue beating. Once mixed, sift in flour (for cake). Beat with hand mixer until sticky.

Make pattern

2 Add 1 tsp of yolk batter to a separate bowl. Stir in 1/4 tsp of cake flour (pattern).

3 Add 1 tsp of yolk batter to another bowl. Stir in 1/4 tsp of black cocoa powder.

4 In a separate bowl, whisk 1 egg white with hand mixer. Add a pinch of corn starch to finish and continue whisking until stiff peaks form.

5 Stir 3 Tbsp of meringue into batter from step **2** (white batter). Stir 3 Tbsp of meringue into batter from step **3** (brown batter). Add both batters to separate cornets.

6 Pipe dots on lined baking sheet with white cornet. Repeat with brown cornet. Bake for 1 minute.

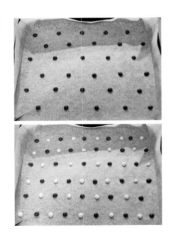

Whisk meringue and make cake batter

7 Gradually add diluted red food coloring to remaining batter from step **1** and stir thoroughly until pink.*

8 Add 4 egg whites to a bowl and beat with hand mixer. Once soft peaks form, whisk in remaining sugar from step **1** (30 g). Once glossy, add remaining corn starch (1 light tsp) and whisk until stiff peaks form.

9 Combine remaining meringue from steps **4** and **8** and stir 1/3 at a time into batter from step **7**. Stir thoroughly until smooth, with no meringue lumps.

10 Pour batter over pre-baked pattern on baking sheet. Smooth out surface. Whack sheet against work surface several times to remove air bubbles.

Bake

11 Bake at 340°F (170°C) for 14 minutes or until done. Cover surface of cake with parchment paper. Flip baking sheet containing cake over onto a cooling rack. Remove sheet.

12 Peel parchment paper from surface right away, then replace paper and allow to cool slightly.

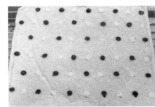

Make filling and roll up

13 Filling: Add sugar to cream and whip until thickened. Cut fruit.

14 Syrup: Dissolve granulated sugar in hot water. Add Kirsch once cooled.

15 Flip cake over onto parchment paper so pattern is on the bottom. Slice off front and back edges of cake at an angle. Lightly score surface of cake at 2 cm (3/4") intervals. Baste with syrup. Spread filling onto cake from the back edge.

16 Arrange fruit on cake. Lift up front edge of cake along with parchment paper and roll forward over fruit. Press firmly and continue to roll up. Refrigerate cake for at least 1 hour.

*If you add all the food coloring at once the color may end up too dark. Stir in gradually and stop once the desired color is achieved.

Arabesque Deco★Cake

**Use green tea powder to color the cake without food coloring.
The flavor perfectly suits the design of this cake.
Use Japanese-style red bean paste for the filling. (Pattern on p 81)**

Prep

- ★ Measure out all ingredients.
- ★ Place paper pattern on baking sheet. Top with parchment paper and lightly grease with oil-soaked paper towel.
- ★ Preheat oven to 340°F (170°C).
- ★ Make cornet out of parchment paper (see p 9).

Ingredients (yields one 25 x 25 cm (appx 10 x 10") cake)

★ Batter

Eggs 4
   Divide into 1 white, 3 whites, and 3 yolks. Discard 1 yolk.
Sugar....................... 1/3 C (65 g)
Water ....3 1/3 Tbsp (50 ml)
Vegetable oil ....2 3/4 Tbsp (40 ml)
Dash vanilla extract

Cake flour (cake)..... 2/3 C (80 g)
Cake flour (pattern).........1/2 tsp
Corn starch ....1 tsp
Maccha green tea powder ....2 tsp
   Dissolve in 1 1/3 Tbsp (20 ml) hot water

★ Syrup

Granulated sugar .... 2 1/2 tsp (10 g)
Hot water...... 1 1/3 Tbsp (20 ml)

★ Filling

Fresh cream .... 2/3 C (150 ml)
Sugar..................... 3 1/3 tsp (14 g)
Sweet boiled azuki beans
.... 1/3 C (70 g)

Make yolk batter

1 Add 3 egg yolks to bowl and whisk. Add half of sugar (35 g) and beat with hand mixer until lighter in color. Add water, oil and vanilla (in that order) and continue beating. Once mixed, sift in flour (for cake). Beat with hand mixer until sticky.

Make pattern

2 Add 1 Tbsp of yolk batter to a separate bowl. Stir in 1/2 tsp of cake flour (pattern).

3 In a separate bowl, whisk 1 egg white with hand mixer. Add a pinch of corn starch to finish and continue whisking until stiff peaks form.

4 Stir 2/3 of meringue into batter from step **2**. Add batter to cornet.

5 On lined baking sheet, pipe arabesque pattern with cornet. Since the lines are thin, make sure they have height.

6 Bake for 1 1/2 minutes.

Whisk meringue and make cake batter

7 Stir dissolved green tea into remaining batter from step **1**.

8 Add 3 egg whites to a bowl and beat with hand mixer. Once soft peaks form, whisk in remaining sugar from step **1** (30 g). Once glossy, add remaining corn starch (1 light tsp) and whisk until stiff peaks form.

9 Combine remaining meringue from steps **3** and **8** and stir 1/3 at a time into batter from step **7**. Stir thoroughly until smooth, with no meringue lumps.

10 Pour batter over pre-baked pattern on baking sheet. Smooth out surface. Whack sheet against work surface several times to remove air bubbles.

Bake

11 Bake at 340°F (170°C) for 14 minutes or until done. Cover surface of cake with parchment paper. Flip baking sheet containing cake over onto a cooling rack. Remove sheet.

12 Peel parchment paper from surface right away, then replace paper and allow to cool slightly.

Make filling and roll up

13 Filling: Add sugar to cream and whip until thickened.

14 Syrup: Dissolve granulated sugar in hot water.

15 Flip cake over onto parchment paper so pattern is on the bottom. Slice off front and back edges of cake at an angle. Lightly score surface of cake at 2 cm (3/4") intervals. Baste with syrup. Spread filling onto cake from the back edge.

16 Arrange azuki beans on cake. Lift up front edge of cake along with parchment paper and roll forward. Press firmly and continue to roll up. Refrigerate cake for at least 1 hour.

Argyle Deco★Cake

The trick to making this argyle pattern pop is to use both light and dark green.
Use simple whipped cream filling to enhance the green tea flavor.
Use red food dye instead of green tea to make a pink arglye version.
(Pattern on p 80)

Prep

★ Measure out all ingredients.
★ Place paper pattern on baking sheet. Top with parchment paper
  and lightly grease with oil-soaked paper towel.
★ Preheat oven to 340ºF (170ºC).
★ Make 2 cornets out of parchment paper (see p 9).

Ingredients (yields one 25 x 25 cm (appx 10 x 10") cake)

★ **Batter**
Eggs 4
  Divide into 1 white, 3 whites,
  and 3 yolks. Discard 1 yolk.
Sugar...................... 1/3 C (65 g)
Water ....3 1/3 Tbsp (50 ml)
Vegetable oil....2 3/4 Tbsp (40 ml)
Dash vanilla extract

Cake flour (cake)..... 2/3 C (80 g)
Cake flour (pattern).........1/2 tsp
Corn starch ....1 tsp
Maccha green tea powder ....2 tsp
  Dissolve in 1 1/3 Tbsp (20 ml)
  hot water

★ **Syrup**
Granulated sugar .... 2 1/2 tsp (10 g)
Hot water...... 1 1/3 Tbsp (20 ml)

★ **Filling**
Fresh cream .... 2/3 C (150 ml)
Sugar..................... 3 1/3 tsp (14 g)

Make yolk batter

1 Add 3 egg yolks to bowl and whisk. Add half of sugar (35 g) and beat with hand mixer until lighter in color. Add water, oil and vanilla (in that order) and continue beating. Once mixed, sift in flour (for cake). Beat with hand mixer until sticky.

Make pattern

2 Add 2 tsp of yolk batter to a separate bowl. Stir in 1/2 tsp of cake flour (pattern).

3 Add 1 tsp of yolk batter to another bowl. Stir in 1 tsp of green tea to make dark green batter.

4 In a separate bowl, whisk 1 egg white with hand mixer. Add a pinch of corn starch to finish and continue whisking until stiff peaks form.

5 Stir 1/3 of meringue into batter from step **2**. Add to a cornet.

6 Stir 3 Tbsp of meringue into batter from step **3**. Add to other cornet.

7 On lined baking sheet, pipe lines with white cornet. Since the lines are thin, make sure they have height. Bake for 1 minute.

8 Pipe diamonds over white lines with dark green cornet. Bake for 1 minute.

Whisk meringue and make cake batter

9 Stir remaining dissolved green tea into batter from step **1**.

10 Add 3 egg whites to a bowl and beat with hand mixer. Once soft peaks form, whisk in remaining sugar from step **1** (30 g). Once glossy, add remaining corn starch (1 light tsp) and whisk until stiff peaks form.

11 Combine remaining meringue from steps **4** and **10** and stir 1/3 at a time into batter from step **9**. Stir thoroughly until smooth, with no meringue lumps.

12 Pour batter over pre-baked pattern on baking sheet. Smooth out surface. Whack sheet against work surface several times to remove air bubbles.

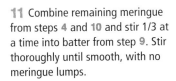

Bake

13 Bake at 340°F (170°C) for 14 minutes or until done. Cover surface of cake with parchment paper. Flip baking sheet containing cake over onto a cooling rack. Remove sheet.

14 Peel parchment paper from surface right away, then replace paper and allow to cool slightly.

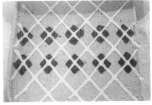

Make filling and roll up

15 Filling: Add sugar to cream and whip until thickened.

16 Syrup: Dissolve granulated sugar in hot water.

17 Flip cake over onto parchment paper so pattern is on the bottom. Slice off front and back edges of cake at an angle. Lightly score surface of cake at 2 cm (3/4") intervals. Baste with syrup. Spread filling thickly onto cake from the back edge.

18 Lift up front edge of cake along with parchment paper and roll forward. Press firmly and continue to roll up. Refrigerate cake for at least 1 hour.

Prep

★ Measure out all ingredients.
★ Place paper pattern on baking sheet. Top with parchment paper and lightly grease with oil-soaked paper towel.
★ Preheat oven to 340°F (170°C).
★ Make 2 cornets out of parchment paper (see p 9).

Ingredients
(yields one 25 x 25 cm (appx 10 x 10") c

★ Batter
Eggs 4
   Divide into 1 white, 3 whites, and 3 yolks. Discard 1 yolk.
Sugar.........................1/3 C (65 g)
Water ....1/4 C (60 ml)
Vegetable oil...... 2 3/4 Tbsp (40 ml)
Dash vanilla extract
Cake flour (cake)........1/2 C (70 g)
Cake flour (pattern)........... 1/2 tsp
Corn starch .... 1 tsp
Cocoa powder (cake) .....2 Tbsp (10 g)
Cocoa powder (pattern) .... 1/2 tsp
....
★ Syrup
Granulated sugar ....2 1/2 tsp (10 g)
Hot water.........1 1/3 Tbsp (20 ml)
Rum .... 1 tsp
....
★ Filling
Fresh cream ....2/3 C (150 ml)
Dark chocolate (bar or squares)
.... 2 1/2 oz (70 g)
Banana....................................... 1

Variation

**Pink Stripes &
Dots Deco Cake**
Draw dots with
black cocoa powder,
top with stripes in plain
batter, then finish with
pink cake batter.

Stripes & Dots Deco★Cake

This is the design I came up with when I wanted a pattern that would be enticing even when cut into pieces for serving. It's fun coming up with new color combinations, too.

Make yolk batter

1 Add 3 egg yolks to bowl and whisk. Add half of sugar (35 g) and beat with hand mixer until lighter in color. Add water, oil and vanilla (in that order) and continue beating. Once mixed, sift in flour. Beat with hand mixer until sticky.

Make pattern

2 Add 1 tsp of yolk batter to a separate bowl. Stir in 1/2 tsp of cocoa powder (for pattern) to make brown batter. Add 1 Tbsp of yolk batter to another bowl. Stir in 1/2 tsp cake flour (for pattern) to make white batter.

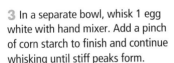

3 In a separate bowl, whisk 1 egg white with hand mixer. Add a pinch of corn starch to finish and continue whisking until stiff peaks form.

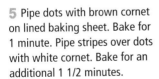

4 Stir 3 Tbsp of meringue into brown batter from step **2**. Add to a cornet. Stir 1/2 of remaining meringue into white batter from step **2**. Add to other cornet.

5 Pipe dots with brown cornet on lined baking sheet. Bake for 1 minute. Pipe stripes over dots with white cornet. Bake for an additional 1 1/2 minutes.

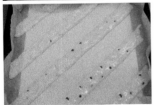

Whisk meringue and make cake batter

6 Sift cocoa (for cake) into remaining yolk batter from step **1**. Stir thoroughly.

7 Add 3 egg whites to a bowl and beat with hand mixer. Once soft peaks form, whisk in remaining sugar from step **1** (30 g). Once glossy, add remaining corn starch (1 light tsp) and whisk until stiff peaks form.

8 Combine remaining meringue from steps **3** and **7** and stir into cocoa batter 1/3 at a time. Stir thoroughly until smooth, with no meringue lumps.

9 Pour batter over pre-baked pattern on baking sheet. Smooth out surface. Whack sheet against work surface several times to remove air bubbles.

Bake

10 Bake at 340°F (170°C) for 14 minutes or until done. Cover surface of cake with parchment paper. Flip baking sheet containing cake over onto a cooling rack. Remove sheet.

11 Peel parchment paper from surface right away, then replace paper and allow to cool slightly.

Make filling and roll up

12 Filling: Finely chop chocolate and melt in double boiler. Combine with cream. Whip with hand mixer until thickened.

13 Syrup: Dissolve granulated sugar in hot water. Add rum once cooled.

14 Flip cake over onto parchment paper so pattern is on the bottom. Slice off front and back edges of cake at an angle. Lightly score surface of cake at 2 cm (3/4") intervals. Baste with syrup. Spread filling onto cake from the back edge.

15 Arrange banana on cake. Lift up front edge of cake along with parchment paper and roll forward over banana. Press firmly and continue to roll up. Refrigerate cake for at least 1 hour.

Strawberry Deco★Cake

These strawberries might look like they're difficult to create,
but you simply bake the red berries then paint on the seeds and stems.
It's very easy.

Variation
Cherries

Draw two circles with pink batter on the baking sheet and draw stems with black cocoa dissolved in hot water.

Prep

★ Measure out all ingredients.
★ Line baking sheet with parchment paper and lightly grease with oil-soaked paper towel.
★ Preheat oven to 340°F (170°C). ★ Prep fine brush (see p 9).
★ Make cornet out of parchment paper (see p 9).

Ingredients (yields one 25 x 25 cm (appx 10 x 10') cake)

★ Batter

Eggs 4
    Divide into 1 white, 3 whites, and 3 yolks. Discard 1 yolk.
Sugar.........................1/3 C (65 g)
Water.......................1/4 C (60 ml)
Vegetable oil....2 3/4 Tbsp (40 ml)
Dash vanilla extract

Cake flour (cake)..... 2/3 C (80 g)
Cake flour (pattern).........1/2 tsp
Corn starch .... 1 tsp
Red food coloring............1/8 tsp
    Dilute with appx 1/4 tsp water

★ Syrup

Granulated sugar .... 2 1/2 tsp (10 g)
Hot water...... 1 1/3 Tbsp (20 ml)
Kirsch .... 1/2 Tbsp

★ Filling

Fresh cream .... 2/3 C (150 ml)
Sugar.....................3 1/3 tsp (14 g)
Strawberries.................about 10

★ Drawing

Black cocoa powder........1/2 tsp
Maccha green tea powder
.... 1/2 tsp
    Dissolve each in 1 tsp hot water

Make yolk batter

1 Add 3 egg yolks to bowl and whisk. Add half of sugar (35 g) and beat with hand mixer until lighter in color. Add water, oil and vanilla (in that order) and continue beating. Once mixed, sift in flour (for cake). Beat with hand mixer until sticky.

Make pattern

2 Add 1 tsp of yolk batter to a separate bowl. Stir in 1/2 tsp of flour (for pattern).

3 Gradually add diluted red food coloring to batter from step **2** until pink in color.

4 In a separate bowl, whisk 1 egg white with hand mixer. Add a pinch of corn starch to finish and continue whisking until stiff peaks form.

5 Stir 3 Tbsp of meringue into pink batter from step **3**. Add to cornet.

6 Pipe strawberries with cornet onto lined baking sheet. Bake for 1 minute.

Whisk meringue and make cake batter

7 Add 3 egg whites to a bowl and beat with hand mixer. Once soft peaks form, whisk in remaining sugar from step **1** (30 g). Once glossy, add remaining corn starch (1 light tsp) and whisk until stiff peaks form.

8 Combine remaining meringue from steps **4** and **7** and stir 1/3 at a time into batter from step **1**. Stir thoroughly until smooth, with no meringue lumps.

9 Pour batter over pre-baked pattern on baking sheet. Smooth out surface. Whack sheet against work surface several times to remove air bubbles.

Bake

10 Bake at 340°F (170°C) for 14 minutes or until done. Cover surface of cake with parchment paper. Flip baking sheet containing cake over onto a cooling rack. Remove sheet.

11 Peel parchment paper from surface right away, then replace paper and allow to cool slightly.

Make filling and roll up

12 Filling: Add sugar to cream and whip until thickened. Quarter strawberries.

13 Syrup: Dissolve granulated sugar in hot water. Add Kirsch once cooled.

14 Flip cake over onto parchment paper so pattern is on the bottom. Slice off front and back edges of cake at an angle. Lightly score surface of cake at 2 cm (3/4") intervals. Baste with syrup. Spread filling onto cake from the back edge.

15 Arrange strawberry slices on cake as shown. Lift up front edge of cake with parchment paper and roll forward over strawberries. Press firmly and continue to roll up. Refrigerate cake for at least 1 hour. To finish, dissolve black cocoa powder in hot water and paint seeds. Dissolve green tea in hot water and paint stems.

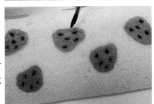

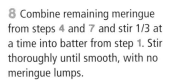

Skull & Bones Deco★Cake

This is the pattern I came up with in response to a request for a design that boys would enjoy. Also makes a very chic gift. (Pattern p 82)

Prep

★ Measure out all ingredients.
★ Place paper pattern on baking sheet. Top with parchment paper and lightly grease with oil-soaked paper towel.
★ Preheat oven to 340°F (170°C).
★ Make cornet out of parchment paper (see p 9).

Ingredients (yields one 25 x 25 cm (appx 10 x 10") cake)

★ Batter

Eggs 4
    Divide into 1 white, 3 whites, and 3 yolks. Discard 1 yolk.
Sugar...................... 1/3 C (65 g)
Vegetable oil....2 3/4 Tbsp (40 ml)
Dash vanilla extract

Coffee A

⌐ Instant coffee................ 2 tsp
| Hot water........ 2 Tbsp (30 ml)
⌐ Milk .... 2 Tbsp (30 ml)
  Dissolve coffee in hot water, then add milk
Cake flour (cake)........2/3 C (80 g)
Cake flour (pattern)............1/2 tsp
Corn starch ....1 tsp

Coffee B

⌐ Instant coffee............... 1 tsp
| Hot water................... 1/2 tsp
  Add 1/2 tsp hot water to instant coffee and stir with rubber spatula until dissolved.

★ Syrup

Granulated sugar .... 2 1/2 tsp (10 g)
Hot water...... 1 1/3 Tbsp (20 ml)
Instant coffee..................... 1 tsp

★ Filling

Fresh cream .... 2/3 C (150 ml)
Sugar..................... 3 1/3 tsp (14 g)

Make yolk batter

1 Add 3 egg yolks to bowl and whisk. Add half of sugar (35 g) and beat with hand mixer until lighter in color. Add Coffee A, oil and vanilla (in that order) and continue beating. Once mixed, sift in flour (for cake). Beat with hand mixer until sticky.

Make pattern

2 Add 2 tsp of yolk batter to a separate bowl. Stir in 1/2 tsp flour (for pattern).

3 Stir in Coffee B to bowl from step **2** to make dark brown batter.

4 In a separate bowl, whisk 1 egg white with hand mixer. Add a pinch of corn starch to finish and continue whisking until stiff peaks form.

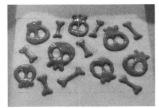

5 Stir 1/3 of meringue into batter from step **3**. Add to cornet.

6 Pipe skull and bones with cornet onto lined baking sheet. Bake for 1 minute.

Whisk meringue and make cake batter

7 Add 3 egg whites to a bowl and beat with hand mixer. Once soft peaks form, whisk in remaining sugar from step **1** (30 g). Once glossy, add remaining corn starch (1 light tsp) and whisk until stiff peaks form.

8 Combine remaining meringue from steps **4** and **7** and stir 1/3 at a time into batter from step **1**. Stir thoroughly until smooth, with no meringue lumps.

9 Pour batter over pre-baked pattern on baking sheet. Smooth out surface. Whack sheet against work surface several times to remove air bubbles.

Bake

10 Bake at 340°F (170°C) for 14 minutes or until done. Cover surface of cake with parchment paper. Flip baking sheet containing cake over onto a cooling rack. Remove sheet.

11 Peel parchment paper from surface right away, then replace paper. While still warm, place in a ziplock bag, seal* and let cool slightly.

Make filling and roll up

12 Filling: Add sugar to cream and whip until thickened.

13 Syrup: Dissolve granulated sugar and instant coffee in hot water. Let cool.

14 Flip cake over onto parchment paper so pattern is on the bottom. Slice off front and back edges of cake at an angle. Lightly score surface of cake at 2 cm (3/4") intervals. Baste with syrup. Spread filling onto cake from the back edge.

15 Lift up front edge of cake along with parchment paper and roll forward. Press firmly and continue to roll up. Refrigerate cake for at least 1 hour.

*Since coffee cake crumbles easily, cooling in a plastic bag retains moisture.

Bunny Deco★Cake

**For these bunnies with a slight Japanese-style flair,
bake the white silhouettes then paint on the red parts to finish.
If the Year of the Rabbit is coming up, make this cake for New Years, too.
(Pattern on p 82)**

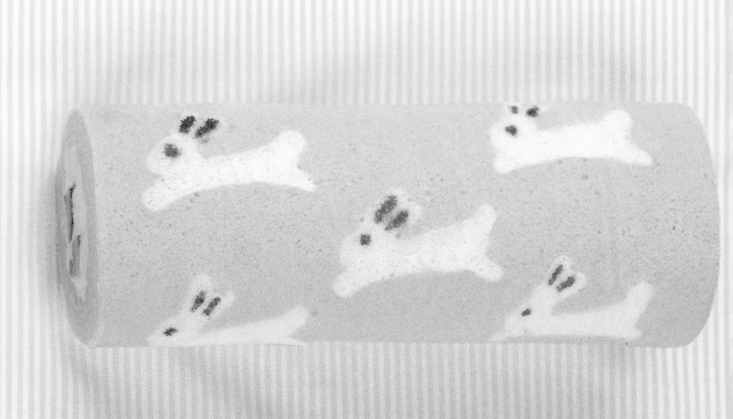

Prep

- ★ Measure out all ingredients.
- ★ Place paper pattern on baking sheet. Top with parchment paper
  and lightly grease with oil-soaked paper towel.
- ★ Preheat oven to 340ºF (170ºC).   ★ Prep fine brush (see p 9).
- ★ Make cornet out of parchment paper (see p 9).

Ingredients (yields one 25 x 25 cm (appx 10 x 10") cake)

★ Batter

Eggs 5	Cake flour (cake)..... 2/3 C (80 g)
Divide into 1 white, 4 whites,	Cake flour (pattern).........1/2 tsp
and 1 yolk. Discard 4 yolks.	Corn starch ....1 tsp
Sugar......................5 Tbsp (60 g)	Red food coloring............1/8 tsp
Water.....................1/4 C (60 ml)	Dilute with appx 1/4 tsp
Vegetable oil..........3 Tbsp (45 ml)	water
Dash vanilla extract	

★ Syrup

Granulated sugar .... 2 1/2 tsp (10 g)
Hot water......1 1/3 Tbsp (20 ml)
Kirsch .... 1/2 Tbsp

★ Filling

Fresh cream .... 2/3 C (150 ml)
Sugar......................3 1/3 tsp (14 g)
Strawberries.................about 10

Make yolk batter

1 Add 1 egg yolk to bowl and whisk. Add half of sugar (30 g) and half of oil (1 1/2 Tbsp) and beat with hand mixer until lighter in color. Add water, remaining oil and vanilla (in that order) and continue beating. Once mixed, sift in flour (for cake). Beat with hand mixer until sticky.

Make pattern

2 Add 2 tsp of yolk batter to a separate bowl. Stir in 1/2 tsp of cake flour (pattern).

3 In a separate bowl, whisk 1 egg white with hand mixer. Add a pinch of corn starch to finish and continue whisking until stiff peaks form.

4 Stir 1/3 of meringue into batter from step **2**. Add to cornet.

5 Pipe bunny shapes on lined baking sheet with cornet. Bake for 1 1/2 minutes.

Whisk meringue and make cake batter

6 Gradually add diluted red food coloring to remaining batter from step **1** and stir thoroughly until pink.*

7 Add 4 egg whites to a bowl and beat with hand mixer. Once soft peaks form, whisk in remaining sugar from step **1** (30 g). Once glossy, add remaining corn starch (1 light tsp) and whisk until stiff peaks form.

8 Combine remaining meringue from steps **3** and **7** and stir 1/3 at a time into batter from step **6**. Stir thoroughly until smooth, with no meringue lumps.

9 Pour batter over pre-baked pattern on baking sheet. Smooth out surface. Whack sheet against work surface several times to remove air bubbles.

Bake

10 Bake at 340°F (170°C) for 14 minutes or until done. Cover surface of cake with parchment paper. Flip baking sheet containing cake over onto a cooling rack. Remove sheet.

11 Peel parchment paper from surface right away, then replace paper and allow to cool slightly.

Make filling and roll up

12 Filling: Add sugar to cream and whip until thickened. Cut strawberries.

13 Syrup: Dissolve granulated sugar in hot water. Add Kirsch once cooled.

14 Flip cake over onto parchment paper so pattern is on the bottom. Slice off front and back edges of cake at an angle. Lightly score surface of cake at 2 cm (3/4") intervals. Baste with syrup. Spread filling onto cake from the back edge.

15 Arrange strawberries on cake. Lift up front edge of cake along with parchment paper and roll forward. Press firmly and continue to roll up. Refrigerate cake for at least 1 hour. Use remaining red food coloring to paint on eyes and ears with brush.

*If you add all the food coloring at once the color may end up too dark. Stir in gradually and stop once the desired color is achieved.

Ladybug Deco★Cake

**They say ladybugs bring good luck. Can this cake do the same?
If you want to simplify this pattern, just eliminate the leaf.
(Pattern on p 83)**

Prep

★ See instructions for other Deco Cakes.

Ingredients (yields one 25 cm² (10"²) cake)

★ Batter
Eggs 4
   Divide into 1 white, 3
   whites, and 3 yolks.
   Discard 1 yolk.
Sugar....... 1/3 C (65 g)
Water.... 1/4 C (60 ml)
Vegetable oil
   ......2 3/4 Tbsp (40 ml)
Dash vanilla extract
Flour (cake) ......2/3 C (80 g)
Flour (pattern).....1 light tsp
Corn starch ....1 tsp
Red food coloring.....1/8 tsp
   Dilute with appx 1/4
   tsp water
Green tea powder....1/4 tsp
Dissolve in 1/2 tsp hot water

★ Syrup
Granulated sugar
..........2 1/2 tsp (10 g)
Hot water
......1 1/3 Tbsp (20 ml)
Kirsch .... 1/2 Tbsp

★ Filling
Fresh cream
.... 2/3 C (150 ml)
Sugar
..........3 1/3 tsp (14 g)
Strawberries
.....................about 10

★ Drawing
Black cocoa powder...1/2 tsp
Dissolve in 1 tsp hot water

Make yolk batter

1 Add 3 egg yolks to bowl and whisk. Add half of sugar (35 g) and beat with hand mixer until lighter in color. Add water, oil and vanilla (in that order) and continue beating. Once mixed, sift in flour (for cake). Beat with hand mixer until sticky.

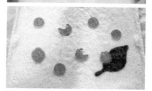

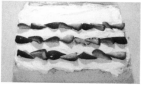

Make pattern

2 Add 1 tsp of yolk batter to 2 separate bowls.

3 Stir in 1/2 tsp of flour and dissolved green tea to 1 bowl from step **2** to make green batter. Stir in 1/4 tsp of flour and gradually add diluted red food coloring to other bowl to make dark pink batter.

4 In a separate bowl, whisk 1 egg white with hand mixer. Add a pinch of corn starch to finish and continue whisking until stiff peaks form.

5 Stir 3 Tbsp of meringue into both green and pink batters. Add both batters to separate cornets.

6 Pipe ladybugs with pink cornet onto lined baking sheet. Bake for 1 minute.

7 Pipe leaf with green cornet onto lined baking sheet. Bake for 1 minute.

Whisk meringue and make cake batter

8 Add 3 egg whites to a bowl and beat with hand mixer. Once soft peaks form, whisk in remaining sugar from step **1** (30 g). Once glossy, add remaining corn starch (1 light tsp) and whisk until stiff peaks form.

9 Combine remaining meringue from steps **4** and **8** and stir 1/3 at a time into yolk batter from step **1**. Stir thoroughly until smooth, with no meringue lumps.

10 Pour batter over pre-baked pattern on baking sheet. Smooth out surface. Whack sheet against work surface several times to remove air bubbles.

Bake

11 Bake at 340ºF (170ºC) for 14 minutes or until done. Cover surface of cake with parchment paper. Flip baking sheet containing cake over onto a cooling rack. Remove sheet.

12 Peel parchment paper from surface right away, then replace paper and allow to cool slightly.

Make filling and roll up

13 Filling: Add sugar to cream and whip until thickened. Cut strawberries.

14 Syrup: Dissolve granulated sugar in hot water. Add Kirsch once cooled.

15 Flip cake over onto parchment paper so pattern is on the bottom. Slice off front and back edges of cake at an angle. Lightly score surface of cake at 2 cm (3/4 ")intervals. Baste with syrup. Spread filling onto cake from the back edge.

16 Arrange strawberry slices on cake as shown. Lift up front edge of cake along with parchment paper and roll forward over strawberries. Press firmly and continue to roll up. Refrigerate cake for at least 1 hour. To finish, dissolve black cocoa powder in hot water and paint on ladybugs' spots.

The Basic:
Wrap in clear plastic and fix with a ribbon!

1 Wrap cake in a sheet of cellophane wider than the cake itself and use cellophane tape to close. Try to keep tape on the bottom of the cake.

2 Fold down excess cellophane sheet on both ends of cake and tape closed.

3 Once cake is completely wrapped up, tie a ribbon around the center.

4 Top with a sticker of your choice. Done!

Use wrapping to dress up cakes even more adorably!

Deco Cakes won't crumble easily and are very handy to carry, making them perfect for gift giving. Here I'll introduce wrapping techniques that show off the cake patterns to greatest advantage.

Stack ribbons for a more fashionable display.

Wrap cake with a wide ribbon then top with a skinny ribbon for a very classy presentation. Ribbons of similar colors give a chic, sophisticated feel while contrasting colors add a vivid dimension. Use lace for a romantic flair.

Color combinations are important!

Half-size cakes are best for smaller gifts.

For casual gifts or a simple thank-you, try cutting a full Swiss roll in half. Try combining two halves of different cakes and you've got a surefire hit.

When making sets, use matching ribbons and stickers.

Combine cakes for 10x the cuteness!

Wrap individual servings so everyone gets a slice!

For times when you want to give gifts to many people, slice up the cakes into individual servings and wrap separately beforehand. Add pink ribbons and these will make perfect friendly Valentines!

Wrap each slice in cellophane and seal with a sticker!

Cellophane

Cellophane is a thin sheet of clear plastic film. It's waterproof and non-breathable, making it ideal for use in wrapping pastries. Can be found in confectionery stores or online in sheet or bag form.

Seasonal and Holiday Deco ★ Cakes

Birthdays, Children's Day, Christmas, etc...
Make Deco Cakes that reflect the season when friends and
loved ones gather for parties.
Aside from lighting up the dinner table, these cakes can be
made with friends or your kids for a fun group activity.

Doll Festival Deco★Cake

**Bake the peach blossoms then paint on the leaves to finish.
If serving at a party, add decorations to make this even more gorgeous
(see p 62 for decoration ideas).
(Pattern on p 83)**

Prep

- ★ Measure out all ingredients.
- ★ Place paper pattern on baking sheet. Top with parchment paper
  and lightly grease with oil-soaked paper towel.
- ★ Preheat oven to 340°F (170°C).   ★ Prep fine brush (see p 9).
- ★ Make 2 cornets out of parchment paper (see p 9).

Ingredients (yields one 25 x 25 cm (appx 10 x 10") cake)

★ Batter

Eggs 4
    Divide into 1 white, 3 whites,
    and 3 yolks. Discard 1 yolk.
Sugar..........................1/3 C (65 g)
Water ....1/4 C (60 ml)
Vegetable oil....2 3/4 Tbsp (40 ml)
Dash vanilla extract

Cake flour (cake)..... 2/3 C (80 g)
Cake flour (pattern).... 1 light tsp
Corn starch .... 1 tsp
Red food coloring............ 1/8 tsp
    Dilute with appx 1/4 tsp
    water

★ Syrup

Granulated sugar .... 2 1/2 tsp (10 g)
Hot water...... 1 1/3 Tbsp (20 ml)
Kirsch .... 1/2 Tbsp

★ Filling

Fresh cream .... 2/3 C (150 ml)
Sugar.................3 1/3 tsp (14 g)
Strawberries.................about 10

★ Drawing

Maccha green tea powder
.... 1/2 tsp
    Dissolve in 1 tsp hot water

Make yolk batter

1 Add 3 egg yolks to bowl and whisk. Add half of sugar (35 g) and beat with hand mixer until lighter in color. Add water, oil and vanilla (in that order) and continue beating. Once mixed, sift in flour (for cake). Beat with hand mixer until sticky.

Make pattern

2 Add 1 tsp of yolk batter to a separate bowl. Stir in 1/4 tsp of flour (for pattern).

3 Add 2 tsp of yolk batter to another bowl. Stir in 1/2 tsp of flour (for pattern) and gradually add diluted red food coloring until pink in color.

4 In a separate bowl, whisk 1 egg white with hand mixer. Add a pinch of corn starch to finish and continue whisking until stiff peaks form.

5 Stir 3 Tbsp of meringue into batter from step **2**. Add to a cornet. Stir 1/3 of meringue into pink batter from step **3**. Add to other cornet.

6 Pipe pistil dots with white cornet onto lined baking sheet. Bake for 1 minute.

7 Pipe flower petals with pink cornet over pistil dots. Bake for 1 minute.

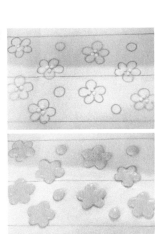

Whisk meringue and make cake batter

8 Add 3 egg whites to a bowl and beat with hand mixer. Once soft peaks form, whisk in remaining sugar from step **1** (30 g). Once glossy, add remaining corn starch (1 light tsp) and whisk until stiff peaks form.

9 Combine remaining meringue from steps **4** and **8** and stir 1/3 at a time into batter from step **1**. Stir thoroughly until smooth, with no meringue lumps.

10 Pour batter over pre-baked pattern on baking sheet. Smooth out surface. Whack sheet against work surface several times to remove air bubbles.

Bake

11 Bake at 340°F (170°C) for 14 minutes or until done. Cover surface of cake with parchment paper. Flip baking sheet containing cake over onto a cooling rack. Remove sheet.

12 Peel parchment paper from surface right away, then replace paper and allow to cool slightly.

Make filling and roll up

13 Filling: Add sugar to cream and whip until thickened. Quarter strawberries.

14 Syrup: Dissolve granulated sugar in hot water. Add Kirsch once cooled.

15 Flip cake over onto parchment paper so pattern is on the bottom. Slice off front and back edges of cake at an angle. Lightly score surface of cake at 2 cm (3/4") intervals. Baste with syrup. Spread filling onto cake from the back edge.

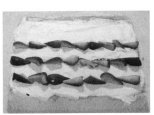

16 Arrange strawberry slices on cake as shown. Lift up front edge of cake along with parchment paper and roll forward over strawberries. Press firmly and continue to roll up. Refrigerate cake for at least 1 hour. To finish, dissolve green tea in hot water and paint leaves.

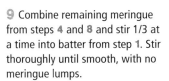

Children's Day Deco★Cake

I took advantage of the long, narrow shape of Swiss roll cakes to
recreate the carp banners that are flown for Children's Day in Japan.
Even a single cake is plenty festive. (Pattern on p 84)

Prep

- ★ Measure out all ingredients.
- ★ Place paper pattern on baking sheet. Top with parchment paper and lightly grease with oil-soaked paper towel.
- ★ Preheat oven to 340°F (170°C). ★ Prep fine brush (see p 9). ★ Make 2 cornets out of parchment paper (see p 9).

Ingredients (yields one 25 x 25 cm (appx 10 x 10") cake)

★ **Batter**

Eggs 4
   Divide into 1 white, 3 whites,
   and 3 yolks. Discard 1 yolk.
Sugar.........................1/3 C (65 g)
Water ....1/4 C (60 ml)
Vegetable oil....2 3/4 Tbsp (40 ml)

Dash vanilla extract
Cake flour (cake)..... 2/3 C (80 g)
Cake flour (pattern).... 1 heaping tsp
Corn starch .... 1 tsp
Red food coloring............ 1/8 tsp
   Dilute with appx 1/4 tsp water
   *Use blue food coloring for
   the blue carp banner.

★ **Syrup**

Granulated sugar .... 2 1/2 tsp (10 g)
Hot water...... 1 1/3 Tbsp (20 ml)
Grand Marnier .... 1/2 Tbsp

★ **Filling**

Fresh cream .... 2/3 C (150 ml)
Sugar.................3 1/3 tsp (14 g)
Kiwi, banana................ 1/4 each
Canned yellow peach.......1 slice

★ **Drawing**

Black cocoa powder ....1/2 tsp
   Dissolve in 1 tsp hot water

Make yolk batter

1 Add 3 egg yolks to bowl and whisk. Add half of sugar (35 g) and beat with hand mixer until lighter in color. Add water, oil and vanilla (in that order) and continue beating. Once mixed, sift in flour (for cake). Beat with hand mixer until sticky.

Make pattern

2 Add 1 tsp of yolk batter to a separate bowl. Stir in 1/4 tsp of flour (for pattern).

3 Add 2 Tbsp of yolk batter to another bowl. Stir in 1 tsp of flour (for pattern).

4 Gradually add diluted red food coloring to batter from step **2** until light pink in color. Add slightly more red food coloring to batter from step **3** until dark pink in color.

5 In a separate bowl, whisk 1 egg white with hand mixer. Add a pinch of corn starch to finish and continue whisking until stiff peaks form.

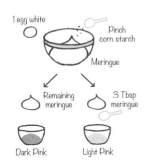

6 Stir 3 Tbsp of meringue into light pink batter. Add to a cornet. Stir remaining meringue into dark pink batter. Add to other cornet.

7 Pipe carp scale pattern with light pink cornet. Bake for 1 minute. Pipe main carp pattern with dark pink cornet. Bake for an additional 1 1/2 minutes.

Whisk meringue and make cake batter

8 Add 3 egg whites to a bowl and beat with hand mixer. Once soft peaks form, whisk in remaining sugar from step 1 (30 g). Once glossy, add remaining corn starch (1 light tsp) and whisk until stiff peaks form.

9 Stir meringue 1/3 at a time into batter from step **1**. Stir thoroughly until smooth, with no meringue lumps.

10 Pour batter over pre-baked pattern on baking sheet. Smooth out surface. Whack sheet against work surface several times to remove air bubbles.

Bake

11 Bake at 340°F (170°C) for 14 minutes or until done. Cover surface of cake with parchment paper. Flip baking sheet containing cake over onto a cooling rack. Remove sheet.

12 Peel parchment paper from surface right away, then replace paper and allow to cool slightly.

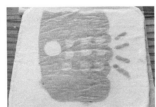

Make filling and roll up

13 Filling: Add sugar to cream and whip until thickened. Cut fruit.

14 Syrup: Dissolve granulated sugar in hot water. Add Grand Marnier once cooled.

15 Flip cake over onto parchment paper so pattern is on the bottom. Slice off front and back edges of cake at an angle. Lightly score surface of cake at 2 cm (3/4") intervals. Baste with syrup. Spread filling onto cake from the back edge.

16 Arrange fruit on cake as shown. Lift up front edge of cake along with parchment paper and roll forward over fruit. Press firmly and continue to roll up. Refrigerate cake for at least 1 hour. To finish, dissolve black cocoa powder in hot water and paint edges of scales and eyes.

Mother's Day Deco★Cake

The trick to making the flowers look like carnations is the light pink inner frilly petals. Feel free to paint on the stems instead of baking them into the cake. (Pattern on p 85)

Prep

- ★ **Measure out all ingredients.**
- ★ **Place paper pattern on baking sheet. Top with parchment paper and lightly grease with oil-soaked paper towel.**
- ★ **Preheat oven to 340°F (170°C).**   ★ **Prep fine brush (see p 9).**
- ★ **Make 3 cornets out of parchment paper (see p 9).**

Ingredients (yields one 25 x 25 cm (appx 10 x 10") cake)

★ Batter
Eggs 4
   Divide into 1 white, 3 whites,
   and 3 yolks. Discard 1 yolk.
Sugar.........................1/3 C (65 g)
Water ....1/4 C (60 ml)
Vegetable oil....2 3/4 Tbsp (40 ml)
Dash vanilla extract

Cake flour (cake)..... 2/3 C (80 g)
Cake flour (pattern)............1 tsp
Corn starch ....1 tsp
Red food coloring............1/8 tsp
   Dilute with appx 1/4 tsp water
Maccha green tea powder
....1/2 tsp
   Dissolve in 1 tsp hot water

★ Syrup
Granulated sugar .... 2 1/2 tsp (10 g)
Hot water......1 1/3 Tbsp (20 ml)
Kirsch .... 1/2 Tbsp

★ Filling
Fresh cream .... 2/3 C (150 ml)
Sugar.................3 1/3 tsp (14 g)
Strawberries.................about 10

★ Lettering
Black cocoa powder........1/2 tsp
   Dissolve in 1 tsp hot water

Make yolk batter

1 Add 3 egg yolks to bowl and whisk. Add half of sugar (35 g) and beat with hand mixer until lighter in color. Add water, oil and vanilla (in that order) and continue beating. Once mixed, sift in flour (for cake). Beat with hand mixer until sticky.

Make pattern

2 Add 2 tsp of yolk batter to 3 separate bowls. Stir in 1/2 tsp of flour (for pattern) to 2 of the 3 bowls.

3 Add green tea to the bowl without additional flour from step **2**. Gradually add diluted red food coloring to 2nd bowl until light pink in color. Add slightly more coloring to the 3rd bowl to create dark pink batter.

4 In a separate bowl, whisk 1 egg white with hand mixer. Add a pinch of corn starch to finish and continue whisking until stiff peaks form.

5 Stir 1/3 of meringue into all 3 batters from step **3**. Add to 3 separate cornets.

6 Pipe inner petals with light pink cornet onto lined baking sheet. Pipe stems and leaves with green cornet. Bake for 1 minute.

7 Pipe outer petals with dark pink cornet over inner petals. Bake for 1 minute.

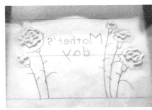

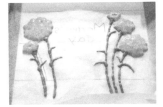

Whisk meringue and make cake batter

8 Add 3 egg whites to a bowl and beat with hand mixer. Once soft peaks form, whisk in remaining sugar from step **1** (30 g). Once glossy, add remaining corn starch (1 light tsp) and whisk until stiff peaks form.

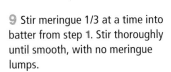

9 Stir meringue 1/3 at a time into batter from step **1**. Stir thoroughly until smooth, with no meringue lumps.

10 Pour batter over pre-baked pattern on baking sheet. Smooth out surface. Whack sheet against work surface several times to remove air bubbles.

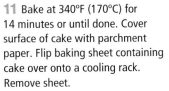
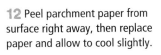

Bake

11 Bake at 340ºF (170ºC) for 14 minutes or until done. Cover surface of cake with parchment paper. Flip baking sheet containing cake over onto a cooling rack. Remove sheet.

12 Peel parchment paper from surface right away, then replace paper and allow to cool slightly.

Make filling and roll up

13 Filling: Add sugar to cream and whip until thickened. Quarter strawberries.

14 Syrup: Dissolve granulated sugar in hot water. Add Kirsch once cooled.

15 Flip cake over onto parchment paper so pattern is on the bottom. Slice off front and back edges of cake at an angle. Lightly score surface of cake at 2 cm (3/4") intervals. Baste with syrup. Spread filling onto cake from the back edge.

16 Arrange strawberry slices on cake as shown. Lift up front edge of cake along with parchment paper and roll forward over strawberries. Press firmly and continue to roll up. Refrigerate cake for at least 1 hour. To finish, dissolve black cocoa powder in hot water and paint Mother's Day message.

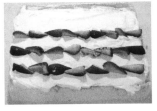

Birthday Deco★Cake

**I designed this cake to reflect a birthday party filled with balloons.
Why not try making blue balloons for a boy's birthday cake?
(Pattern on p 85)**

Prep

- ★ Measure out all ingredients.
- ★ Place paper pattern on baking sheet. Top with parchment paper and lightly grease with oil-soaked paper towel.
- ★ Preheat oven to 340ºF (170ºC).   ★ Prep fine brush (see p 9).
- ★ Make 2 cornets out of parchment paper (see p 9).

Ingredients (yields one 25 x 25 cm (appx 10 x 10") cake)

★ Batter

Eggs 4
   Divide into 1 white, 3 whites, and 3 yolks. Discard 1 yolk.
Sugar...........................1/3 C (65 g)
Water ....1/4 C (60 ml)
Vegetable oil....2 3/4 Tbsp (40 ml)
Dash vanilla extract

Cake flour (cake)..... 2/3 C (80 g)
Cake flour (pattern)............ 1 tsp
Corn starch .... 1 tsp
Red food coloring........... 1/8 tsp
   Dilute with appx 1/4 tsp water

★ Syrup

Granulated sugar .... 2 1/2 tsp (10 g)
Hot water...... 1 1/3 Tbsp (20 ml)
Kirsch .... 1/2 Tbsp

★ Filling

Fresh cream .... 2/3 C (150 ml)
Sugar...................3 1/3 tsp (14 g)
Strawberries.............................4
Kiwi.......................................1/4
Banana..................................1/2

★ Lettering

Black cocoa powder........ 1/2 tsp
   Dissolve in 1 tsp hot water

Make yolk batter

1 Add 3 egg yolks to bowl and whisk. Add half of sugar (35 g) and beat with hand mixer until lighter in color. Add water, oil and vanilla (in that order) and continue beating. Once mixed, sift in flour (for cake). Beat with hand mixer until sticky.

Make pattern

2 Add 2 tsp of yolk batter to 2 separate bowls. Stir in 1/2 tsp of flour (for pattern) to both bowls.

3 Gradually add diluted red food coloring to 1 bowl from step **2** until light pink in color. Add slightly more coloring to the other bowl from step **2** to create dark pink batter.

4 In a separate bowl, whisk 1 egg white with hand mixer. Add a pinch of corn starch to finish and continue whisking until stiff peaks form.

5 Stir 1/3 of meringue into both batters from step **3**. Add to separate cornets.

6 Pipe small balloons with light pink cornet onto lined baking sheet. Bake for 1 minute.

7 Pipe remaining balloons with dark pink cornet. Pipe polka dots with both pink batters in open spaces. Bake for 1 minute.

Whisk meringue and make cake batter

8 Add 3 egg whites to a bowl and beat with hand mixer. Once soft peaks form, whisk in remaining sugar from step **1** (30 g). Once glossy, add remaining corn starch (1 light tsp) and whisk until stiff peaks form.

9 Combine remaining meringue from steps **4** and **8** and stir 1/3 at a time into batter from step **1**. Stir thoroughly until smooth, with no meringue lumps.

10 Pour batter over pre-baked pattern on baking sheet. Smooth out surface. Whack sheet against work surface several times to remove air bubbles.

Bake

11 Bake at 340°F (170°C) for 14 minutes or until done. Cover surface of cake with parchment paper. Flip baking sheet containing cake over onto a cooling rack. Remove sheet.

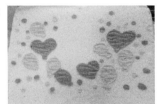

12 Peel parchment paper from surface right away, then replace paper and allow to cool slightly.

Make filling and roll up

13 Filling: Add sugar to cream and whip until thickened. Cut fruit.

14 Syrup: Dissolve granulated sugar in hot water. Add Kirsch once cooled.

15 Flip cake over onto parchment paper so pattern is on the bottom. Slice off front and back edges of cake at an angle. Lightly score surface of cake at 2 cm (3/4") intervals. Baste with syrup. Spread filling onto cake from the back edge.

16 Arrange fruit slices on cake as shown. Lift up front edge of cake along with parchment paper and roll forward over fruit. Press firmly and continue to roll up. Refrigerate cake for at least 1 hour. To finish, dissolve black cocoa powder in hot water and paint birthday message.

Try adding "Deco Toppings" using cream and fruit!

Deco Cakes are plenty adorable all on their own, but if you've got the energy and inclination, try adding Deco Toppings.
Dress up the cakes with whipped cream and fruit for very lovely variations.

Top with a hearty helping of fruit

Add whipped cream to a piping bag and squeeze on top of the cake. Top with slices of the same fruit used inside the cake for visual balance. Garnish with mint or chervil for an extra pretty touch.

Baste bananas with sugar water to keep from oxidizing.

Even more gorgeous!

Make simple shapes with decorating pens

Fill a decorating pen with melted chocolate pastels, draw simple shapes on parchment paper, chill for 30 seconds to harden then peel off paper and add to cake. Try adding colors like pink and white for a showy presentation.

Lovely!

You can use multiple colors if they're the same as the cake colors without it looking messy.

Cut strawberries into hearts for topping

Remove strawberry stems with V-shaped cuts to create hearts and brush with nappage (clear jelly glaze for pastries). This extra step makes strawberries glossy and all the more tempting.

Add mint leaves to contrast with the red of the fruit for a more vivid impression.

Use store-bought decorations

Top cake with whipped cream and fruit then garnish with commercial decorative picks for a more polished look. Add cake candles for even more cuteness.

Pipe whipped cream into flower shapes for an added touch of liveliness.

This is the life of the party!

Add a decorative *mizuhiki* knot to a homemade cake

Top the cake with colorful cookies and add a decorative celebratory knot for a Japanese-style New Year's edible decoration. Garnish with a sprinkling of gold flakes.

Serve this gorgeous Deco Cake during New Year's celebrations!

Make chocolate decorations

Melt chocolate squares in a double boiler, add to a cornet and pipe shapes on parchment paper. Since cornets hold more volume than decorating pens, pipe out thickly to create 3D shapes. Deliciousness is guaranteed.

Use the same design as the pattern on the cake for an extra layer of cuteness.

Even sliced up cakes look so cute!

Once sliced for serving, the surface pattern is difficult to see, but adding Deco Toppings maintains the showiness of the presentation. I recommend toppings for when you mess up the pattern or end up with air bubbles in the cake.

Keep in mind cuts will be made every inch or so when adding toppings.

It's fine wherever you cut!

Fireworks Deco★Cake

Pink and white fireworks blast off against a summer night sky of chocolate cake.

Prep

★ See instructions for other Deco Cakes.

Ingredients (yields one 25 cm² (10"²) cake)

★ Batter	★ Syrup
Eggs 4	Granulated sugar
Divide into 1 white, 3	...........2 1/2 tsp (10 g)
whites, and 3 yolks.	Hot water
Discard 1 yolk.	......1 1/3 Tbsp (20 ml)
Sugar.......1/3 C (65 g)	Rum ....1 tsp
Water....1/4 C (60 ml)	
Vegetable oil	★ Filling
......2 3/4 Tbsp (40 ml)	Fresh cream
Dash vanilla extract	...........2/3 C (150 ml)
Flour (cake)...1/2 C (70 g)	Sugar
Flour (pattern)..........1 tsp	...........3 1/3 tsp (14 g)
Corn starch ....1 tsp	Banana.....................1
Red food coloring.....1/8 tsp	
Dilute with appx 1/4	
tsp water	
Cocoa powder...2 Tbsp (10 g)	

Make yolk batter

1 Add 3 egg yolks to bowl and whisk. Add half of sugar (35 g) and beat with hand mixer until lighter in color. Add water, oil and vanilla (in that order) and continue beating. Once mixed, sift in flour. Beat with hand mixer until sticky.

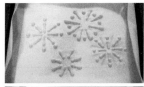

Make pattern

2 Add 2 tsp of yolk batter to a separate bowl. Stir in 1/2 tsp of flour.

3 Add another 2 tsp of yolk batter to another bowl. Stir in 1/2 tsp of cake flour. Gradually add diluted red food coloring until light pink in color.

4 In a separate bowl, whisk 1 egg white with hand mixer. Add a pinch of corn starch to finish and continue whisking until stiff peaks form.

5 Stir 1/3 of meringue into the batter from step **2** (for white batter). Stir 1/3 of meringue into the batter from step **3** (for pink batter). Add both batters to separate cornets.

6 Pipe fireworks (8 lines radiating from the center) with pink cornet onto lined baking sheet. Bake for 1 minute.

7 Pipe radiating lines with white cornet between pink firework lines on baking sheet. Bake for 1 minute.

Whisk meringue and make cake batter

8 Sift cocoa into remaining batter from step **1**. Stir thoroughly.

9 Add 3 egg whites to a bowl and beat with hand mixer. Once soft peaks form, whisk in remaining sugar from step **1** (30 g). Once glossy, add remaining corn starch (1 light tsp) and whisk until stiff peaks form.

10 Combine remaining meringue from steps **4** and **9** and stir into cocoa batter 1/3 at a time. Stir thoroughly until smooth, with no meringue lumps.

11 Pour batter over pre-baked pattern on baking sheet. Smooth out surface. Whack sheet against work surface several times to remove air bubbles.

Bake

12 Bake at 340ºF (170ºC) for 14 minutes or until done. Cover surface of cake with parchment paper. Flip baking sheet containing cake over onto a cooling rack. Remove sheet.

13 Peel parchment paper from surface right away, then replace paper and allow to cool slightly.

Make filling and roll up

14 Filling: Add sugar to cream and whip until thickened.

15 Syrup: Dissolve granulated sugar in hot water. Add rum once cooled.

16 Flip cake over onto parchment paper so pattern is on the bottom. Slice off front and back edges of cake at an angle. Lightly score surface of cake at 2 cm (3/4") intervals. Baste with syrup. Spread filling onto cake from the back edge.

17 Arrange banana on cake. Lift up front edge of cake along with parchment paper and roll forward over banana. Press firmly and continue to roll up. Refrigerate cake for at least 1 hour.

Prep

★ **See instructions for other Deco Cakes.**

Ingredients (yields one 25 cm² (10"²) cake)

★ Batter

Eggs 4
  Divide into 1 white, 3 whites, and 3 yolks. Discard 1 yolk.
Sugar....... 1/3 C (65 g)
Water .... 1/4 C (60 ml)
Vegetable oil ......2 3/4 Tbsp (40 ml)
Dash vanilla extract
Cake flour (cake) .... 2/3 C (80 g)
Corn starch ....1 tsp
Black cocoa powder ....1 tsp

★ Syrup

Granulated sugar ....2 1/2 tsp (10 g)
Hot water ......1 1/3 Tbsp (20 ml)
Grand Marnier .... 1/2 Tbsp

★ Filling

Fresh cream ....2/3 C (150 ml)
Sugar...3 1/3 tsp (14 g)
Canned yellow peach ....1 slice
Canned white peach ....1 slice

Recital Deco ★ Cake

In order to keep all the symbols facing the right direction once the cake is flipped over, I made the pattern a mirror image. (Pattern on p 86)

Make yolk batter

1 Add 3 egg yolks to bowl and whisk. Add half of sugar (35 g) and beat with hand mixer until lighter in color. Add water, oil and vanilla (in that order) and continue beating. Once mixed, sift in flour (for cake). Beat with hand mixer until sticky.

Make pattern

2 Add 2 tsp of yolk batter to a separate bowl. Stir in 1 tsp black cocoa powder.

3 In a separate bowl, whisk 1 egg white with hand mixer. Add a pinch of corn starch to finish and continue whisking until stiff peaks form.

4 Stir 1/3 of meringue into batter from step **2**. Add to cornet.

5 On lined baking sheet, pipe musical pattern with cornet. Bake for 1 minute.

Whisk meringue and make cake batter

6 Add 3 egg whites to a bowl and beat with hand mixer. Once soft peaks form, whisk in remaining sugar from step **1** (30 g). Once glossy, add remaining corn starch (1 light tsp) and whisk until stiff peaks form.

7 Combine remaining meringue from steps **3** and **6** and stir 1/3 at a time into batter from step **1**. Stir thoroughly until smooth, with no meringue lumps.

8 Pour batter over pre-baked pattern on baking sheet. Smooth out surface. Whack sheet against work surface several times to remove air bubbles.

Bake

9 Bake at 340ºF (170ºC) for 14 minutes or until done. Cover surface of cake with parchment paper. Flip baking sheet containing cake over onto a cooling rack. Remove sheet.

10 Peel parchment paper from surface right away, then replace paper and allow to cool slightly.

Make filling and roll up

11 Filling: Add sugar to cream and whip until thickened. Cut fruit.

12 Syrup: Dissolve granulated sugar in hot water. Add Grand Marnier once cooled.

13 Flip cake over onto parchment paper so pattern is on the bottom. Slice off front and back edges of cake at an angle. Lightly score surface of cake at 2 cm (3/4") intervals. Baste with syrup. Spread filling onto cake from the back edge.

14 Arrange fruit on top of cake. Lift up front edge of cake along with parchment paper and roll forward over fruit. Press firmly and continue to roll up. Refrigerate cake for at least 1 hour.

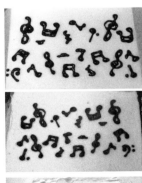

Halloween Deco★Cake

Why not try making an orange and white stripe cake for Halloween?
Combine red and yellow food coloring to produce an orange hue.
(Pattern on p 86)

Prep

- ★ **Measure out all ingredients.**
- ★ **Place paper pattern on baking sheet. Top with parchment paper and lightly grease with oil-soaked paper towel.**
- ★ **Preheat oven to 340°F (170°C).**   ★ **Prep fine brush (see p 9).**
- ★ **Make 2 cornets out of parchment paper (see p 9).**

Ingredients (yields one 25 x 25 cm (appx 10 x 10") cake)

★ Batter

Eggs 4
   Divide into 1 white, 3 whites,
   and 3 yolks. Discard 1 yolk.
Sugar .... 1/3 C (65 g)
Water .... 1/4 C (60 ml)
Vegetable oil .... 2 3/4 Tbsp (40 ml)
Dash vanilla extract

Cake flour (cake) ..... 2/3 C (80 g)
Cake flour (pattern) .... 1 tsp
Corn starch .... 1 tsp
Red food coloring .... 1/8 tsp
Yellow food coloring .... 1/8 tsp
   Dilute with appx 1/4 tsp water
Black cocoa powder .... 1 tsp

★ Syrup

Granulated sugar .... 2 1/2 tsp (10 g)
Hot water ...... 1 1/3 Tbsp (20 ml)
Rum .... 1 tsp

★ Filling

Fresh cream .... 2/3 C (150 ml)
Dark chocolate (bar or squares)
.... 2 1/2 oz (70 g)
Banana 1

★ Lettering

Black cocoa powder .... 1/2 tsp
   Dissolve in 1 tsp hot water

Make yolk batter

1 Add 3 egg yolks to bowl and whisk. Add half of sugar (35 g) and beat with hand mixer until lighter in color. Add water, oil and vanilla (in that order) and continue beating. Once mixed, sift in flour. Beat with hand mixer until sticky.

Make pattern

2 Add 1 Tbsp of yolk batter to 2 separate bowls.

3 Stir in 1 tsp of cocoa powder to one of the bowls from step **2** to make brown batter. Stir in 1 tsp cake flour (for pattern) and gradually stir in red and yellow food coloring to make orange batter.

4 In a separate bowl, whisk 1 egg white with hand mixer. Add a pinch of corn starch to finish and continue whisking until stiff peaks form.

5 Stir 1/2 of meringue into both batters from step **3**. Add each batter to separate cornets.

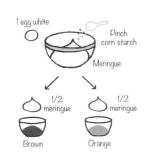

6 Pipe jack-o-lantern and bat with brown cornet on lined baking sheet. Bake for 1 minute.

7 Pipe stripes with orange cornet. Bake for an additional 1 1/2 minutes.

Whisk meringue and make cake batter

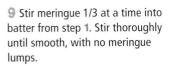

8 Add 3 egg whites to a bowl and beat with hand mixer. Once soft peaks form, whisk in remaining sugar from step **1** (30 g). Once glossy, add remaining corn starch (1 light tsp) and whisk until stiff peaks form.

9 Stir meringue 1/3 at a time into batter from step **1**. Stir thoroughly until smooth, with no meringue lumps.

10 Pour batter over pre-baked pattern on baking sheet. Smooth out surface. Whack sheet against work surface several times to remove air bubbles.

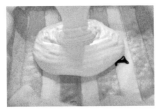

Bake

11 Bake at 340°F (170°C) for 14 minutes or until done. Cover surface of cake with parchment paper. Flip baking sheet containing cake over onto a cooling rack. Remove sheet.

12 Peel parchment paper from surface right away, then replace paper and allow to cool slightly.

Make filling and roll up

13 Filling: Finely chop chocolate and melt in double boiler. Combine with cream. Whip with hand mixer until thickened.

14 Syrup: Dissolve granulated sugar in hot water. Add rum once cooled.

15 Flip cake over onto parchment paper so pattern is on the bottom. Slice off front and back edges of cake at an angle. Lightly score surface of cake at 2 cm (3/4") intervals. Baste with syrup. Spread filling onto cake from the back edge.

16 Arrange banana on cake. Lift up front edge of cake along with parchment paper and roll forward over banana. Press firmly and continue to roll up. Refrigerate cake for at least 1 hour. To finish, dissolve black cocoa powder in hot water and paint Halloween message on cake.

Christmas Deco★Cake

Take on the challenge of a cake pattern with three colors for a major event like Christmas. The Christmas wreath is created with dark and light green and red batters. (Pattern on p 87)

Prep

★ **Measure out all ingredients.**
★ **Place paper pattern on baking sheet. Top with parchment paper and lightly grease with oil-soaked paper towel.**
★ **Preheat oven to 340°F (170°C).**   ★ **Prep fine brush (see p 9).**
★ **Make 3 cornets out of parchment paper (see p 9).**

Ingredients (yields one 25 x 25 cm (appx 10 x 10") cake)

★ Batter
Eggs 4
    Divide into 1 white, 3 whites,
    and 3 yolks. Discard 1 yolk.
Sugar..........................1/3 C (65 g)
Water ....1/4 C (60 ml)
Vegetable oil....2 3/4 Tbsp (40 ml)
Dash vanilla extract

Cake flour (cake)..... 2/3 C (80 g)
Cake flour (pattern).........3/4 tsp
Corn starch .... 1 tsp
Red food coloring............1/8 tsp
    Dilute with appx 1/4 tsp water
Maccha green tea powder ...1/2 tsp
    Dissolve in 1 tsp hot water

★ Syrup
Granulated sugar .... 2 1/2 tsp (10 g)
Hot water...... 1 1/3 Tbsp (20 ml)
Kirsch .... 1/2 Tbsp

★ Filling
Fresh cream .... 2/3 C (150 ml)
Sugar.................3 1/3 tsp (14 g)
Strawberries............................4
Kiwi.......................................1/4
Banana.................................1/2

★ Lettering
Black cocoa powder........1/2 tsp
    Dissolve in 1 tsp hot water

Make yolk batter

1 Add 3 egg yolks to bowl and whisk. Add half of sugar (35 g) and beat with hand mixer until lighter in color. Add water, oil and vanilla (in that order) and continue beating. Once mixed, sift in flour (for cake). Beat with hand mixer until sticky.

Make pattern

2 Add 1 tsp of yolk batter to 3 separate bowls. Stir in 1/4 tsp of flour (for pattern) to all 3 bowls.

3 Gradually add diluted red food coloring to 1 bowl from step **2** until red in color. Add a dash of dissolved green tea to 2nd bowl to make light green batter. Add remaining green tea to 3rd bowl to make dark green batter.

4 In a separate bowl, whisk 1 egg white with hand mixer. Add a pinch of corn starch to finish and continue whisking until stiff peaks form.

5 Stir 3 Tbsp of meringue into all 3 batters from step **3**. Add batters to separate cornets.

6 Pipe circles with red cornet onto lined baking sheet. Pipe leaves with dark green cornet. Bake for 1 minute.

7 Pipe remaining leaves with light green cornet. Bake for an additional 1 1/2 minutes.

Whisk meringue and make cake batter

8 Add 3 egg whites to bowl and beat with hand mixer. Once soft peaks form, whisk in remaining sugar from step **1** (30 g). Once glossy, add remaining corn starch (1 light tsp) and whisk until stiff peaks form.

9 Combine remaining meringue from steps **4** and **8** and stir 1/3 at a time into batter from step **1**. Stir thoroughly until smooth, with no meringue lumps.

10 Pour batter over pre-baked pattern on baking sheet. Smooth out surface. Whack sheet against work surface several times to remove air bubbles.

Bake

11 Bake at 340°F (170°C) for 14 minutes or until done. Cover surface of cake with parchment paper. Flip baking sheet containing cake over onto a cooling rack. Remove sheet.

12 Peel parchment paper from surface right away, then replace paper and allow to cool slightly.

Make filling and roll up

13 Filling: Add sugar to cream and whip until thickened. Cut fruit.

14 Syrup: Dissolve granulated sugar in hot water. Add Kirsch once cooled.

15 Flip cake over onto parchment paper so pattern is on the bottom. Slice off front and back edges of cake at an angle. Lightly score surface of cake at 2 cm (3/4") intervals. Baste with syrup. Spread filling onto cake from the back edge.

16 Arrange fruit on cake as shown. Lift up front edge of cake along with parchment paper and roll forward over fruit. Press firmly and continue to roll up. Refrigerate cake for at least 1 hour. To finish, dissolve black cocoa powder in hot water and paint Christmas message.

Christmas Candle
Deco★Cake

Make 2 thin roll cakes, cut into several lengths then
stand on a serving dish. Top with strawberries that look like
candle flames for a gorgeous presentation.
This is actually easier than making
a layer cake.

Prep

- ★ **Measure out all ingredients.**
- ★ **Line baking sheet with parchment paper and lightly grease with oil-soaked paper towel.**
- ★ **Preheat oven to 340°F (170°C).**
- ★ **Make cornet out of parchment paper (see p 9).**
- ★ **Prep a pastry piping bag with a round metal tip.**

Ingredients (yields one 30 x 30 cm (appx 12 x 12") cake)

★ Batter	★ Syrup
Eggs 4	Granulated sugar ...2 1/2 tsp (10 g)
Divide into 1 white,	Hot water...1 1/3 Tbsp (20 ml)
3 whites, and 3 yolks.	Kirsch ....1/2 Tbsp
Discard 1 yolk.	
Sugar...................5 Tbsp (60 g)	★ Filling
Water .... 1/4 C (60 ml)	Fresh cream .... 1 1/4 C (300 ml)
Vegetable oil...2 3/4 Tbsp (40 ml)	Sugar..................2 Tbsp (24 g)
Dash vanilla extract	Strawberries...........1 package
Cake flour (cake)..2/3 C (80 g)	Blueberries ....15 to 20
Cake flour (pattern)..... 1/2 tsp	Nappage .... as needed
Corn starch .... 1 tsp	Mint leaves .... as needed
Red food coloring........ 1/8 tsp	
Dilute with appx 1/4 tsp	*Nappage is a clear jelly glaze
water	used to give confectionery or
	fruits a glossy look. Sold in
	confectionery stores or online.

*This recipe requires a thinner, larger cake than the others, so prep a 30 x 30 cm (appx 12 x 12") baking sheet.

*If using a 25 x 25 cm (10 x 10") sheet, the cake will be too short and won't roll up to a perfect circle, but you can simply conceal the seams by arranging on the plate so the seams face the inside.

Make yolk batter

1 Add 3 egg yolks to bowl and whisk. Add half of sugar (30 g) and beat with hand mixer until lighter in color. Add water, oil and vanilla (in that order) and continue beating. Once mixed, sift in flour (for cake). Beat with hand mixer until sticky.

Make pattern

2 Add 2 tsp of yolk batter to a separate bowl. Stir in 1/2 tsp of flour (for pattern).

3 Gradually add diluted red food coloring to bowl from step **2** until pink in color.

4 In a separate bowl, whisk 4 egg whites with hand mixer. Once soft peaks form, whisk in remaining sugar from step **1** (30 g). Once glossy, add corn starch (1 tsp) and whisk until stiff peaks form.

5 Stir 1/3 of meringue into batter from step **3**. Add to cornet.

6 Pipe stripes with pink cornet onto lined baking sheet. Bake for 1 minute.

Whisk meringue and make cake batter

7 Stir remaining meringue 1/3 at a time into batter from step **1**. Stir thoroughly until smooth, with no meringue lumps.

Meringue left over from step 4

8 Pour batter over pre-baked pattern on baking sheet. Smooth out surface. Whack sheet against work surface several times to remove air bubbles.

Bake

9 Bake at 340°F (170°C) for 14 minutes or until done. Cover surface of cake with parchment paper. Flip baking sheet containing cake over onto a cooling rack. Remove sheet.

340°F 14 mins

10 Peel parchment paper from surface right away, then replace paper and allow to cool slightly.

Make filling and roll up

11 Filling: Add sugar to cream and whip until soft peaks form. Transfer 1/3 of whipped cream to another bowl (for cake top decoration). Continue to whip remaining cream.

12 Syrup: Dissolve granulated sugar in hot water. Add Kirsch once cooled.

13 Flip cake over onto parchment paper so pattern is on the bottom. Lightly score surface of cake at 2 cm (3/4") intervals. Slice cake in half lengthwise to create 2 slender roll cakes.

14 Baste both cakes with syrup. Spread filling onto cakes from back edges.

15 Reserve 6 strawberries for cake top decorations. Remove stems and quarter remaining strawberries.

16 Arrange quartered strawberries on top of cream-covered cake.

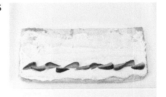

17 Lift up front edge of cake along with parchment paper and roll forward over strawberries. Press firmly and continue to roll up. Repeat with other cake. Refrigerate cake for at least 1 hour.

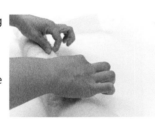

Decorate

18 Cut both roll cakes into 3 to 4 pieces of varying lengths. Keep under 10 cm (4") long so the cakes will stand up straight when plated.

19 While keeping the height balance in mind, arrange cut cakes on plate so the seams face inward.

20 Remove stems from decorative strawberries and glaze with nappage.

21 If needed, re-whip reserved loose whipped cream from step 11. Once thick enough, spoon on top of standing cakes from step 19.

22 Add glazed strawberries on top of whipped cream. These represent the candle flames.

23 Continue whipping leftover cream from step 21 until stiff peaks form and add to pastry piping bag. Pipe whipped cream around base of cakes on the plate. Place remaining strawberry slices in gaps between the cake and cream. Glaze blueberries and mint leave with mappage and arrange on top of cream.

24 Garnish with a Christmas decoration. Done!

New Year's Deco★Cake

**The perfect end to a New Year's celebratory meal is a festive
red-and-white checkered pattern. (See p 63 for decorating ideas.)
(Pattern on p 87)**

Prep

- ★ **Measure out all ingredients.**
- ★ **Place paper pattern on baking sheet. Top with parchment paper
  and lightly grease with oil-soaked paper towel.**
- ★ **Preheat oven to 340°F (170°C).**   ★ **Prep fine brush (see p 9).**
- ★ **Make cornet out of parchment paper (see p 9).**

Ingredients (yields one 25 x 25 cm (appx 10 x 10") cake)

★ Batter

Eggs 4
    Divide into 1 white, 3 whites,
    and 3 yolks. Discard 1 yolk.
Sugar.......................... 1/3 C (65 g)
Water .... 1/4 C (60 ml)
Vegetable oil....2 3/4 Tbsp (40 ml)
Dash vanilla extract

Cake flour (cake)..... 2/3 C (80 g)
Cake flour (pattern)............ 1 tsp
Corn starch .... 1 tsp
Red food coloring............ 1/8 tsp
    Dilute with appx 1/4 tsp water

★ Syrup

Granulated sugar .... 2 1/2 tsp (10 g)
Hot water...... 1 1/3 Tbsp (20 ml)
Grand Marnier .... 1/2 Tbsp

★ Filling

Fresh cream .... 2/3 C (150 ml)
Sugar.................. 3 1/3 tsp (14 g)
Kiwi, banana................ 1/4 each
Canned yellow peach...1 section

★ Lettering

Black cocoa powder........ 1/2 tsp
    Dissolve in 1 tsp hot water

Make yolk batter

1 Add 3 egg yolks to bowl and whisk. Add half of sugar (35 g) and beat with hand mixer until lighter in color. Add water, oil and vanilla (in that order) and continue beating. Once mixed, sift in flour (for cake). Beat with hand mixer until sticky.

3 yolks

1/4 C water

2 3/4 Tbsp oil

1/2 sugar (35 g)

Dash vanilla extract

2/3 C flour

Make pattern

2 Add 2 Tbsp of yolk batter to a separate bowl. Stir in 1 tsp of flour (for pattern).

3 Gradually add diluted red food coloring to batter from step **2** until dark pink in color.

4 In a separate bowl, whisk 1 egg white with hand mixer. Add a pinch of corn starch to finish and continue whisking until stiff peaks form.

5 Stir 2/3 of meringue into pink batter from step **3**. Add to cornet.

2 Tbsp yolk batter

1 tsp flour

Dash red food coloring

1 egg white

Pinch corn starch

Meringue

2/3 meringue

Pink

6 Pipe checks with cornet onto lined baking sheet. Bake for 1 1/2 minutes.

Whisk meringue and make cake batter

7 Add 3 egg whites to bowl and beat with hand mixer. Once soft peaks form, whisk in remaining sugar from step **1** (30 g). Once glossy, add remaining corn starch (1 light tsp) and whisk until stiff peaks form.

3 egg whites

1/2 sugar (30 g)

1 light tsp corn starch

Meringue

Meringue left over from step 4

8 Combine remaining meringue from steps **4** and **7** and stir 1/3 at a time into batter from step **1**. Stir thoroughly until smooth, with no meringue lumps.

9 Pour batter over pre-baked pattern on baking sheet. Smooth out surface. Whack sheet against work surface several times to remove air bubbles.

Bake

340°F 14 mins

10 Bake at 340°F (170°C) for 14 minutes or until done. Cover surface of cake with parchment paper. Flip baking sheet containing cake over onto a cooling rack. Remove sheet.

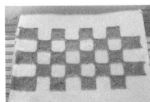

11 Peel parchment paper from surface right away, then replace paper and allow to cool slightly.

Make filling and roll up

12 Filling: Add sugar to cream and whip until thickened. Cut fruits.

13 Syrup: Dissolve granulated sugar in hot water. Add Grand Marnier once cooled.

14 Flip cake over onto parchment paper so pattern is on the bottom. Slice off front and back edges of cake at an angle. Lightly score surface of cake at 2 cm (3/4") intervals. Baste with syrup. Spread filling onto cake from the back edge.

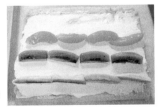

15 Arrange fruit on cake as shown. Lift up front edge of cake along with parchment paper and roll forward over fruit. Press firmly and continue to roll up. Refrigerate cake for at least 1 hour. To finish, dissolve black cocoa powder in hot water and paint New Year's message.

Deco★Cakes Q&A
For Better Baking

I've collected common errors and how to deal with them.
Once you master a few basics you can make cute cakes in no time!

Q Can I do the pattern over if I make a mistake?

A If you haven't yet poured the cake batter on top, you can replace the parchment paper with the pattern and draw it from scratch. If there's a mistake on the pattern after it's baked, cover with whipped cream so you can't see it. Also, patterns will be reversed once baked, so be sure to draw letters and notes backwards.

Q The pattern batter ran after it was baked.

A If you don't pre-bake the pattern well enough, it will run when the cake batter is poured on top or when the sheet is whacked to remove air bubbles. Always pre-bake pattern in a preheated oven. If the pattern still seems too wet after baking for listed time, continue to bake at 30-second intervals until surface is dried, but don't bake for over 3 minutes as pattern will shrink. For best results, the surface should seem slightly dried out.

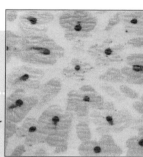

Q The cake looks brown after baking.

A Each oven varies in actual temperature. If the cakes come out browned, try lowering temperature to 320°F (160°C).

Q The pattern stuck to the parchment paper and peeled away from the cake.

A Always be sure to grease the paper before baking. Also, if the lines in the pattern are too fine, there's a greater risk they'll peel away from the cake, so be sure to pipe fairly thick lines.

Q My baking sheet is larger than 25 x 25 cm (10 x 10″)...

A You can use a 30 x 30 cm (12 x 12″) sheet with no problems, but recently specialized Swiss roll cake baking sheets have come onto the market. They're very convenient so I recommend buying one.

Q When I rolled the cake up it cracked.

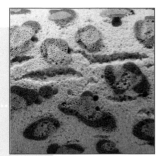

A When you flip the cake over and let it cool slightly, be sure to keep it covered so it doesn't dry out. If it cools completely and dries out, it's more prone to breaking, so the trick is to roll it up while it's still warm.

Q The first parts of the pattern collapsed while I was drawing it.

A The trick is to whip the meringue until stiff peaks form. Keep the egg whites refrigerated until just before whipping. They're easier to whip at room temperature but deflate much faster, too. The addition of corn starch helps retain the aerated texture.

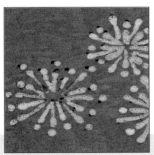

Q I want to serve these to my kids. Do I have to use alcohol in the syrup?

A As there is very little alcohol used, it's OK to use just water and sugar for the syrup. Another option is to boil the sugar, water and liquor in a pan to cook off the alcohol content before serving to children.

Q The baked cake has lots of little holes on the surface.

A If the cake batter isn't thoroughly mixed, air bubbles will form and burst on the surface of the cake during baking. While adding the meringue to the yolk batter be sure to scoop up from the bottom of the bowl and thoroughly incorporate the meringue. Also, don't forget to whack the bottom of the pan before baking to remove air bubbles.

Q I couldn't roll it properly and the cake collapsed.

A If you spread the whipped cream filling on the cake while it's still hot, the cream will melt and the cake will likely collapse. Be sure to wait until the cake has cooled a bit before spreading with cream. Since the cake is a very pliant chiffon cake, it won't roll properly if the whipped cream filling is too loose, so be sure to whip cream until it's very thick.

Q The surface of the cake is all wrinkly.

A Please peel off the parchment paper as soon as you remove the cake from the oven. If you leave it on, moisture that condensed on the paper will cause it to wrinkle and transfer wrinkles to the cake.

How to use patterns

1 Enlarge pattern to 120% before using.

2 Be sure to keep the center line of the pattern near the middle of the pan.

3 Place a sheet of parchment paper over the pattern.

4 Trace pattern with batter and bake.

- You can bake the cake with the paper pattern still underneath.
- Since the ends of the cake will be sliced off before serving, there's no need to draw the pattern all the way to the left and right edges.
- If using a 30 x 30 cm (12 x 12") pan, place center line of paper pattern slightly above the middle of the pan, towards the back edge of the cake.

P26 Teddy Bear ■ Dark Brown ■ Light brown

Enlarge to 120%

Center line ▶

■ White

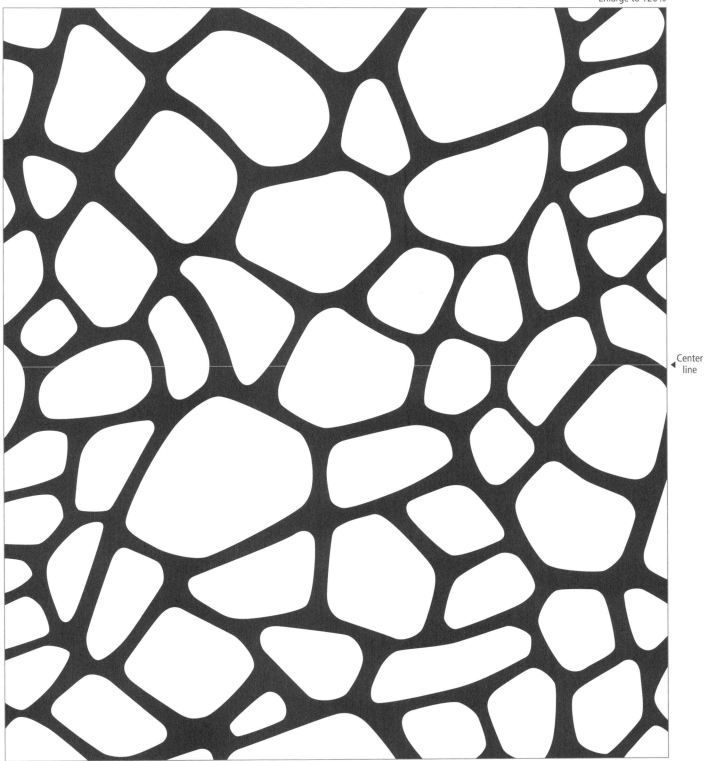

◄ Center line

P30 Dalmatian ■ Dark brown

Enlarge to 120%

Center
line ▶

*Make 2 copies to cover entire baking sheet.

P40 Argyle ■ Dark green ▨ White

Enlarge to 120%

Center
line ▶

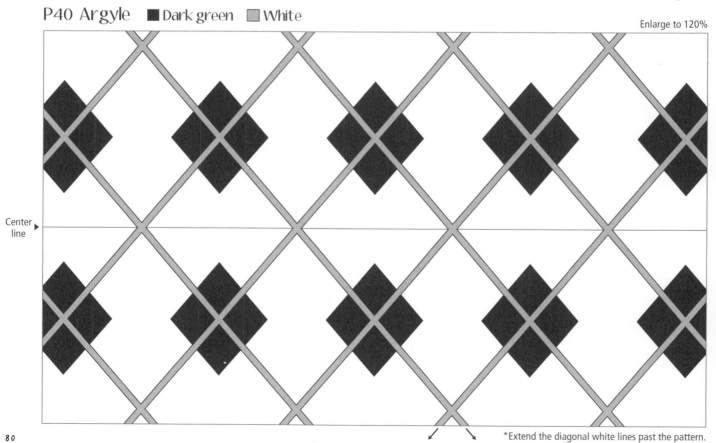

*Extend the diagonal white lines past the pattern.

Center
line

P46 Skull & Bones ■ Dark brown

Center
line ▶

P48 Bunny ■ White

Center
line ▶

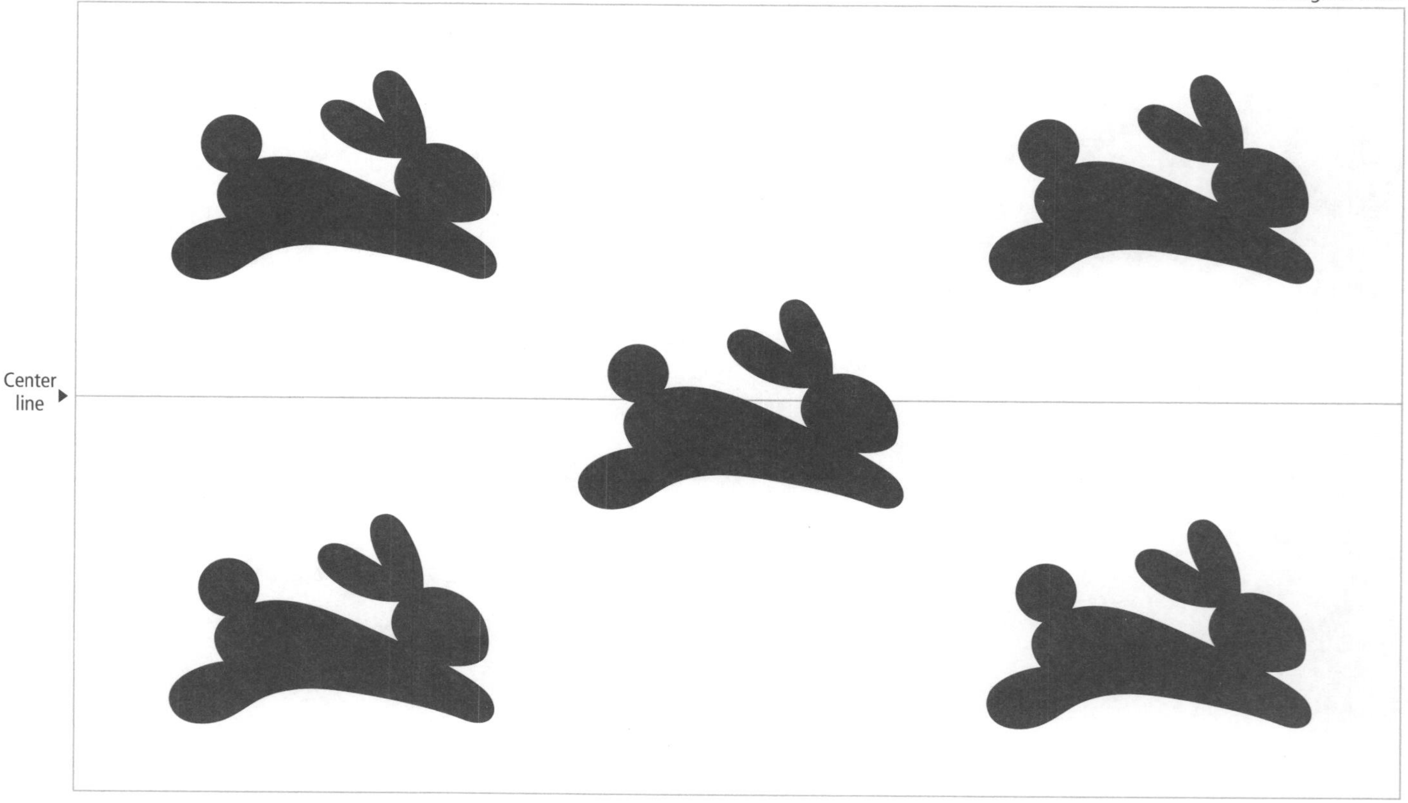

P50 Ladybug ■ Red □ Green

Enlarge to 120%

◄ Center line

P54 Doll Festival ■ Pink □ White

Enlarge to 120%

◄ Center line

Center
line ▶

P58 Mother's Day ■ Green ■ Dark pink □ Light pink

Enlarge to 120%

◄ Center line

P60 Birthday ■ Dark pink □ Light pink

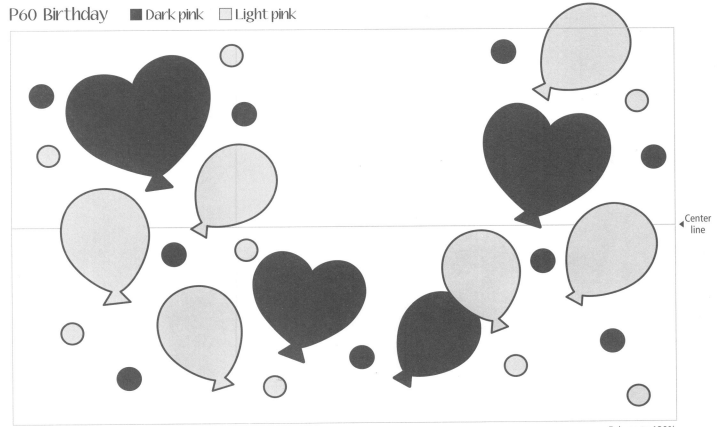

◄ Center line

Enlarge to 120%

P65 Recital ■ Black

Enlarge to 120%

Center line ▶

P66 Halloween ■ Brown ☐ Orange

Enlarge to 120%

Center line ▶

P68 Christmas ■ Dark green ■ Pink □ Light green

Enlarge to 120%

◄ Center line

P74 New Year's ■ Pink

Enlarge to 120%

◄ Center line

87

Junko

Real name: Junko Kato. While working as a graphic designer, she resolved to turn her hobby, baking, into a profession and enrolled in junior college where she majored in human life and sciences with a focus on diet and nutrition. Junko is a food specialist and certified dietician. Thanks to her background as a graphic designer, her specialty is creating confections that pack a powerful visual punch. Her blog, "A Little Extra Effort for Cute Cakes" which she started in 2008, receives over 10,000 hits per day.

Blog: "A Little Extra Effort for Cute Cakes"
http://ameblo.jp/chottono-kufu/
https://www.facebook.com/JunkoDecoroll

Staff

Photography／Yasukazu Nishimura
　　　　　　 Miyu Moriwaki　（P8.P9.P11〜19.P34.P65.P72.P73)

Illustrations／Igloo*dining*

Design／Yuta Nakano（Studio Give)

Editing・Composition／Hatsuko Matsuo

Editing／Eri Fujimoto（Media Factory)

Product Collaboration／Asai Tools
Rakuten Shop: http://www.rakuten.ne.jp/gold/asai-tool/

Special Thanks／Takayuki Kusakabe

Deco★Cakes!
Swiss Rolls for Every Occasion

Translation: Maya Rosewood
Vetting:　 Maria Hostage
Production: Risa Cho
　　　　　 Hiroko Mizuno

Translation provided by Vertical, Inc., 2014
Published by Vertical, Inc., New York

ISBN: 978-1-939130-36-5

Manufactured in the United States of America

First Edition

Vertical, Inc.
451 Park Avenue South, 7th Floor
New York, NY 10016
www.vertical-inc.com